W9-AAT-696

THE Disney PARTY HANDBOOK

14 Fun-Filled Parties!

By Alison Boteler

Disney PRESS

New York

To Thomas and Robby

Photography by Matthew Klein
Food Stylist: Andrea Swenson
Assistant Food Stylist: Amy Lord
Props Stylist: Sheila Shulman
Crafts by Lina Morielli

Text and illustrations © 1998 Disney Enterprises, Inc.
All rights reserved.
No part of this book may be reproduced or transmitted in any form or by any means, electronic or mechanical, including photocopying, recording, or by any information storage and retrieval system, without written permission from the publisher. For information address Disney Press, 114 Fifth Avenue, New York, New York 10011-5690.

Printed in the United States of America.

First Edition
ISBN 0-7394-0039-8

Mr. Potato Head is a registered trademark of Hasbro, Inc. Used with permission. Copyright © 1995 Hasbro, Inc. All rights reserved.

Slinky Dog James Industries. Used with permission. All rights reserved.

Contents

Introduction

Cherish the moment. . . . Every year your child has a unique birthday that only happens once in a lifetime. I remember each and every one of those magical events as if they were yesterday. It was the only day of the year when Mom let me have ice cream for breakfast!

In our hectic world, it's easy to miss the whole point of having birthday parties. They're not about throwing the biggest bash you can possibly afford or buying expensive prizes and party favors. Birthdays are a celebration of your child's life and how precious that is to you. What better way to show this than by creating a party together. By working as a team, parents and kids can create a day of fun and fantasy that both you and your children can enjoy.

The Disney Legacy

Birthday celebrations are one of the most enduring social customs, linking one generation to another. For more than three generations, Disney, with its rich legacy of family entertainment, has become part of the traditions and experiences shared by families throughout the world.

From the first feature-length cartoon, *Snow White and the Seven Dwarfs*, to the revolutionary animation of *Toy Story*, Disney studios has opened windows to worlds no one had ever seen before. In this place of miraculous moving images, anything and everything seems possible.

When you stop and think about it, isn't that what children really need? They need a chance to create their own scenery (without boundaries) and paint it with the colors of their dreams. Fantasy is the realm of endless potential. That's what draws us, our parents, and our children to Disney films. For a brief moment, you can be Pocahontas with the breeze blowing through your hair, you can fly over Agrabah on Aladdin's Magic Carpet, or live like Ariel in a sand castle under the sea.

Choosing a Theme

Obviously, your child's age and interests should be key factors in choosing a party theme. Disney films appeal to a broad range of ages, and so can Disney theme parties. Children appreciate different elements of a party at different levels of maturity (until they finally "outgrow" them, grow up, and then experience them on a whole new level . . . as parents).

Treat food, favors, games, and activities detailed for each party as suggestions to get your own creative juices flowing. As a parent, you'll want to select those elements from any party that are most appropriate to your child's age and personality. Do not hesitate to combine themes or characters. In fact, I've taken the liberty of doing that myself! Sleeping Beauty's Disney Princess Pizza Party brings heroines from favorite films together for a super slumber party. Other parties can be used interchangeably. For example The Hunchback of Notre Dame Party is great for birthdays, Halloween, or a Halloween birthday!

Party-Time Line

Not only do children's interests change as they grow, so do their needs. Keep this in mind when planning any party. I've listed some basic points to remember, dividing them into age categories. Several parties in this book might span two age ranges, meaning you can adjust them to suit your child's peer group. For example, when five-year-olds come to a Winnie the Pooh Party, expect to play the full range of games and activities. If the party is for toddlers, just serve cake and ice cream and play a little ROO TOSS (page 8) while having refreshments with the other parents.

Prime time for Disney parties are probably ages four through eight. Many themes, however, do appeal to older kids with the outside range of nine for boys and eleven for girls.

Ages 1–3: These first parties are a package deal . . . a parent should accompany each child. In this group children need the presence of their parents to keep them calm and content. These birthdays are wonderful opportunities for friends and families to socialize and share child-rearing experiences. Your party preparation efforts are actually more appreciated by the other parents than the kids. Remember that toddler parties should always be visually stimulating and based on simple concepts. The Winnie the Pooh Party, 101 Dalmatians Puppy Party, and the Lion King Party are good choices for this age-group.

Ages 4–5: By now, the birthday party concept has really begun to sink in. Kids understand that everyone gets their own personal holiday when they are considered "reigning monarch." The only problem is that they want it to happen 365 days a year! This can cause stress when some guests really wish your party was theirs. Generally speaking, this age makes an enthusiastic audience. They're ready to be entertained. Keep games short and simple; too many activities will wear kids out. This age-group tires quickly.

Ages 6–7: This is party prime time. Involve your child in as much of the preparation as possible: making invitations and favors, decorating the house, and helping out in the kitchen. This age almost always insists on a full lunch, not just cake and ice cream.

Ages 8–10: This age group takes more effort to impress. At eight, most boys are losing interest in theme parties. Girls gravi-tate almost exclusively to slumber parties. Away-from-home activities become very popular—movies, Rollerblading, and swimming. However, theme food served before or after the outing is by no means "baby stuff." Perhaps childhood lingers longest on Halloween. (Don't we adults know about that!) The idea of dressing in costume and assuming another identity is always irresistible. I still vividly remember my sixth-grade Halloween party. Trick-or-treating had lost its challenge and my parents weren't about to let me participate with the prankster set. That year I made a green satin Scarlet O'Hara costume, and my best friend showed up as a Martian . . . made from the same material! Despite this fashion faux pas, we had a wonderful time.

How Large? How Long?

There are many theories about this. Some say add one guest for each year of your child's age. In a make-believe world this would make an excellent plan. However, when kids reach school age, this is practically impossible.

After years of experience with this issue, I've concluded that, if at all possible, twelve guests should be the maximum party size and is often the ideal number. There are enough children to play team games and create that special aura of party excitement—without too much chaos. You should have at least one adult

present for every three kids up to age seven to help keep things under control. Under age three there should be an adult with every child. Try and limit it to a maximum of six children and six "escorts."

Unfortunately, planning a party's size isn't always a matter of applying a simple formula. Frequently a child feels obliged to invite the entire class to avoid hurt feelings. Also, children may have collected "party payback" obligations throughout the year. When a large party is inevitable, don't panic. Enlist the aid of additional adults and adapt the party accordingly. For instance, with a large group just concentrate on cake and ice cream (doubling recipes as needed).

For very young children, keep the party *short*. An hour is all it takes to work off a little steam and eat cake and ice cream. For structured games, a full lunch, and opening presents—allow two hours.

Shorten extralarge parties to one and one half hours and just serve dessert. It's better to run out of time than run out of things to do. However, always remember to figure in additional drop-off and pick-up time. Children don't all arrive or leave on schedule.

Competing Parties and "Babes of Summer"

Conflicting parties are unavoidable. Regardless of the actual date, every parent wants to celebrate their child's birthday on Saturday afternoon. If two parties are planned for the same day, never let this situation escalate into a popularity contest. As soon as it comes to your attention, phone the other child's parents and try to reach a compromise. If necessary, offer to reschedule your child's party. If this isn't an option, offer to coordinate the parties so that one is in the morning and one is in the afternoon. You might even suggest combining the parties into a double celebration at another location such as a public park. Some parents will actually be eager to share the effort and expense.

Children with summer birthdays are long-suffering. Despite the idyllic weather, friends are often at summer camp or on family vacations. My brother was one of those babes of summer. He envied my May birthday when school was still in session. My brother felt cheated out of presents, much the same as Christmas-birthday kids. There are ways to arrange a consolation party. One would be an "unbirthday party." The date could be the exact day of your child's half-year mark. If that isn't a convenient time either, capitalize on an annual Halloween party.

Documenting the Party

Since the camera was first invented, birthdays have been one of the most important moments to capture on film. Technology never ceases to amaze. As I look at pictures of my fourth birthday, taken on a Brownie snapshot camera, I think: "Then came Polaroid, then came 8mm home movies, and then came camcorders." I write this realizing that what's now state of the art will become obsolete. However, one thing never changes. Whether you're touring Europe or taking pictures of your toddler's first steps, you're not living if you're living behind the camera.

That's not to say those pictures aren't important —they're priceless! But don't miss out on the full experience of these moments. Whenever possible, recruit someone else to take charge of the camera or camcorder. They're more likely to end up with an accurate account of the event. Parents sometimes can't help turning into directors at their own child's party. The event is so important to you that you can stifle the children or end up with staged-looking mug shots. Besides, you have enough to do. You need to relax and enjoy yourself so that your child can, too.

If you must take charge of the camera, be sure it's one you've used before (if not, take some practice shots first).

Check to see that everything's working, that you have enough film and that the batteries aren't dead. Focus on photographing the high points of the party, or those you find especially whimsical, without interrupting the fun.

Party guests also enjoy seeing themselves at their silliest. When costumes are involved, take-home Polaroids mounted in a clever way are treasured keepsakes. Any time games involving acting out a fantasy or storytelling are played, kids love to watch the instant replay. When I was a kid my friends and I spent part of some parties watching home movies of ourselves from the year before. Save your tapes! Many children get a kick out of looking at themselves when they were "just kids"—a year ago.

Opening Presents and Post-Party Depression

Ask any birthday boy or girl and they'll tell you that opening presents is the high point of the party. However, it's not as thrilling for the guests. This can cause problems. Put yourself in the shoes of a child who hands over a gift they'd really like to keep. It's never easy—that's where party favors are supposed to help even the score.

It's a good idea to

prepare your own children for when they're the party-goer rather than the party-giver. Involve children in the gift selection process, but steer them away from toys they "gotta have" themselves.

The best gifts to buy are toys or games your child already owns. This teaches kids how to bond by sharing a mutual interest or experience. Of course, the best lesson of all is the joy of giving, but that can be hard to instill in young children.

As parents of the birthday child, gifts can present problems as well: namely, duplicate presents. Every year has hot toys that become popular birthday gifts. One year, it was inevitable that I would open up five Slinky boxes. By the end of my party there were Slinkies twisted around the crab apple tree and wrapped up the staircase banister. This situation is frustrating for both the giver and the "givee." Not only is the birthday child disappointed when their gift is Beenie Copter number three, so is the child who brought it.

Make sure you review the essentials of etiquette with your child before the party (not during). A birthday host who is polite and gracious, regardless of the gift, will ultimately gain respect from his or her peers.

Some parents adopt the attitude: "No presents opened until everyone's gone home." This strategy usually doesn't

work very well. The ritual of exchanging presents in front of peers has become a childhood rite of passage. Without the presents, the party seems incomplete. The best solution seems to be saving the opening of packages until the end of the party. It prolongs the mystery while postponing broken toys and post-party depression. Every parent knows the signs: The party's over . . . you breathe a sigh of relief, but it's one of the lowest points in your child's life. Kids anticipate their party and presents months in advance. Now it won't happen again for a whole year . . . that can seem like an eternity!

To ease the transition from birthday to "unbirthday," plan to set aside an unopened present (one from you or a relative) for a rainy day. Save a piece of cake in the freezer and surprise your child a few weeks after the party. Anticipating an impromptu birthday encore always brought me back from my post-party blues. Gee . . . Mom was smart!

How to Use This Book

Think of this as a handbook for fantasy, food, and fun. It's not meant to be a manual of official rules to follow. You and your child make up all the rules. If you're short on time, take shortcuts! In certain sections of the book you'll see special hints called *NO TIME? TIPS*.

Every party has been structured with the same format and the same elements: ideas for a homemade invitation, suggestions for decorations, a get-acquainted activity, a fantasy feature, three theme games, and a full lunch menu with cake and ice cream. Apply the same "easy-does-it" philosophy for planning the party's "structure."

Children by nature are unstructured, so don't feel you have to do it all or even the way I say. If you don't have the time or budget to prepare everything on the menu, then don't. If your child wants a favorite food that isn't on the menu, that's what you should serve. If you only have time to make dessert, then just serve cake or ice cream.

One of my favorite chapters in the book is on *ICE-CREAM CREATIONS* (page 190). These scene stealers are always the life of the party. No time to bake a cake? Ice-cream desserts are a snap to make, from MEEKO'S ICE-CREAM RACCOONS (page 197) to the DISNEY ICE-CREAM DREAM CASTLE (page 207). You can even let the kids at the party entertain themselves by making their own.

The instructions and recipes in this book are designed for parties of twelve. Of course, you can always cut the required materials and ingredients for a smaller party, or adjust them for a larger one.

Everything in this book is readily available in your own community. You won't have to seek out specialty cake pans, prizes, or favors. I believe there's a certain whimsy to simplicity. For example, a plain paper bag can be transformed into Muffasa's mane, or pasta can be painted and strung into a Pocahontas-style necklace. Children particularly enjoy creative crafts from common objects.

There's also a wealth of adorable Disney theme products on the market. No doubt, you may want to incorporate these into a party. However, this book is full of do-it-yourself ideas for whenever you and your child want to add a unique, personal touch.

Invitations

A creative party deserves a creative invitation. It's simple to buy them at a stationery store but so much more fun to design your own. If your child is old enough to write, he or she can help make invitations—and get involved in the whole party-planning process.

Homemade invitations are often over-sized, so check your local office-supply store for large envelopes of various dimensions. Be sure to mail (or hand deliver) invitations about two to three weeks before the date of the party. Any earlier than that, parents may forget the date; any later, families may have made other plans. Write "RSVP" on the invitation. That way, you're more likely to hear from everyone than if you simply write "Regrets Only." People tend to forget to regret; no response does not necessarily mean someone is not going to attend. If you're not sure of the party size, the planning process and food preparation can turn into a guessing game.

Decorations

The decorations in each chapter are suggestions and possible inspiration for your own good ideas. Obviously, you'll have to adapt to whether you're holding the party indoors or outdoors. Never feel obligated to go over budget on decorations. You're not designing a Hollywood set! Do what you can with what you have and with the amount of energy you can devote to the project.

It doesn't take much to put kids in the party spirit. Paper goods are readily available at party shops. Some of the big party supply chains have everything for every season—even out of season. Don't forget to capitalize on friends and neighbors as a great resource for borrowing all sorts of oddball stuff. (Just remember to return it!)

Get-Acquainted Activity

It's noon, five children have arrived, and seven more are on the way. What do you do to keep the first arrivals occupied? How do you discourage them from disturbing the food and decorations before the rest of the guests can see them? How do you break the ice and encourage interaction? I consider these first few minutes to be critical—they can set the tone for the whole party.

As soon as the kids start to have a good time, they'll continue to have a good time. That's why I've included a get-acquainted activity for every party in this book. The activity is usually something simple: a craft, costume, or exercise that introduces the guests to the party's theme. It should be something each child can work on either independently or with a small group. This will allow arriving guests to join in without interrupting any "work in progress."

Fantasy Feature

A hat, a favor, or any special treat that each guest takes home as a souvenir can be the fantasy feature of a party. The fantasy feature can also be a key element in the party table decor, such as ARIEL'S TREASURE CHEST (page 38). It can be a hat, as in the case of POOH PALS PARTY HATS (page 5), or it can be edible, like the PIZZA PLANET POPCORN ALIENS (page 79). Whenever you're short on time, or your child is eager to involve friends, consider making the fantasy feature a get-acquainted activity.

Games

Many of the party games in this book have familiar rules. What makes them novel is their connection to classic Disney movies. These encourage kids to identify with their favorite characters and act out the film's fantasy. Every party in this book has three suggested games. (For some reason three games was the magic number at all my childhood parties. It worked well then, and it works well now.)

Just because you see a game in a certain chapter doesn't mean you can't play it in another. My first rule regarding games: Rules are meant to be broken!, at least when it comes to party games. And, I'm not just talking about what games to play at what parties. I've seen many occasions where kids have evolved a game into something else entirely. So what? As long as the children are having fun, isn't that the point of having parties? As I mentioned, most games employ one of several basic dynamics. What follows are some classics.

Types of Tag:

There's always an "it" trying to touch the other players who are avoiding "it."

Examples of tag games would be TIGGER TAG (page 8) or FROLLO'S FROZEN GARGOYLES (page 106).

Hide-and-Seek:

Hide-and-seek games can involve either the players hiding from the seeker such as HERE COMES CRUELLA (page 17), or seekers searching for something hidden by the hider such as HIDE THE HONEY FROM THE HEFFALUMPS (page 6).

Hunting Games:

Similar to an Easter egg hunt, these games have children searching for a hidden object, PETER PAN'S SHADOW HUNT (page 32), or objects, BURIED BONES (page 17).

Passing Games:

These involve children passing around an

object while music is played and then interrupted, or some other definitive moment causes one player to be "stuck" with the object. This child sits out and the circle grows smaller and smaller. Examples of this would be PASS MRS. POTTS (page 65) or HOT POTATO HEAD (page 79).

Musical Chairs: Children circle around chairs to music, until it comes to a stop. There's always one less chair than there is a player. The child left standing sits out, and another chair is removed. Of course, children don't have to sit on chairs. They could sit on mats as in CIRCLE OF LIFE (page 24).

Fishing:
This traditional game requires a fishing pole and hook for kids to pull up prizes or party favors. Prizes are either directly caught with the hook, as in CAPTAIN HOOK'S TREASURE CHEST (page 33) and CLAW MACHINE (page 81), or objects numbering a prize as in STARFISH FISHING (page 39).

Word of Mouth:
This game usually starts with children sitting in a circle and passing a secret message from player to player. According to the "gossip" principle, the message becomes extremely distorted as in THE TWILIGHT BARK (page 15).

Storytelling:
The same circle concept in word of mouth also applies here, although nothing said is secret. One player begins a story and leaves it dangling for the next player to continue. Kids really love embellishing on classics in crazy ways, as with SCARY FAIRY TALEATHON (page 96). ONCE UPON A TIME . . . (page 64) is based on the same principle, only the story is written in a book and passed around.

Relays:
You'll soon see that I love relay games! Even timid children tend to come out of their shell, whether it's a DUST BUNNY DERBY (page 65), MAGIC CARPET RACE (page 71), or CHICAHOMINY RIVER CANOE RACE (page 87). Other games can't compare to the excitement and suspense of two teams racing to finish the same silly goal first.

Note: The only thing that puts a damper on relays is if you let it turn into a replay of picking teams in gym class. It's much better to arbitrarily number off kids on the "eeni-meeni-every-other-one" system.

Expect there to be a poor winner, a poor loser, or even a child who (for whatever reason) is unable to have fun. Because a child's personality traits are often magnified in party settings, be prepared to deal with the problem tactfully. Remember that it's not your role to try and change the children or play psychologist. Just help them adapt as well as possible to the party experience.

Prizes

Although prizes are an essential part of parties, they should be small, simple, inexpensive objects and treats. The fact that a child wins them is what makes them special! Prizes in disguise (wrapped in colored tissue) are much more mysterious and exciting.

Some suggestions to think about are small boxes of crayons, markers, paint kits, combs or brushes, mirrors, whistles, plastic jewelry, bubble pipes, yo-yos, bandannas, bright socks, magnets, rubber balls, pinball puzzles, miniature cars, planes, animals, and of course Disney theme favors. Interesting lollipops, chocolate coins, unusual candies, or popcorn balls make good edible prizes. For a nutritious twist, try wrapping apples, oranges, or boxes of raisins in colored cellophane.

You may not need awards for every game. Some are more activity-oriented. Such games have no definitive ending and, therefore, no clear winner. Other types of games warrant prizes for the entire team.

Winnie the Pooh Party

Winnie the Pooh is the world's favorite bear. We all grew up with Pooh and now want our children to experience that same whimsical world. Pooh's endearing qualities of consideration, humor, and friendship have made him an enduring literary classic. Kids love the idea that he was an almost real-life bear of a real-life boy named Christopher Robin.

English author A. A. Milne created these stories around his own son's collection of stuffed animals, including timid Piglet, bouncy Tigger, and doleful Eeyore. In the '60s Disney produced four feature films based on Milne's classics. Today, Pooh stars in his own Saturday morning cartoon show along with all his friends from the Hundred-Acre Wood. No doubt he'll be as popular with your children's children as he is today.

Invitation

Owl Card

Decorations

Pooh-Style Picnic

Red checkered tablecloth, picnic basket, Pooh plates, graham cracker bears
in honey pots, Christopher Robin's kite-tail napkins, and Piglet balloons

Get-Acquainted Activity

Baby Roo Jelly-Bean Bags

Fantasy Feature

Pooh Pals Party Hats

Eeyore Ears or Piglet Ears

Games

Hide the Honey from the Heffalumps

Tigger Tag

Roo Toss

Menu

Pooh Bear's Biscuit Burgers with Honey Mustard.....118

Orange-Pineapple Owls.....119

Hundred-Acre Wood Honey-Apple Punch.....119

Peanut Butter Pooh Cake.....174

Frozen Tiggers.....194

Invitation

Owl Card

Pooh's friend Owl asks guests to come to a picnic in honor of your child's birthday.

Materials:

6 (9" x 12") sheets poster board
ruler
scissors
carbon paper
black felt-tip pen
light brown and yellow felt-tip markers
12 (5" x 7") envelopes
Yield: 12 invitations

Directions:

1. Cut the sheets into 9" x 6" strips.
2. Fold the strips to form cards that measure 4½" x 6".
3. Transfer the picture of Owl's face onto the front of each card by lightly tracing the pattern on next page.

4. Outline each face with a black felt-tip pen. Fill in the area around the eyes with a light brown felt-tip marker. Color the beak yellow.
5. Underneath Owl's face write the following:

GUESS WHOO'S HAVING
A BIRTHDAY PARTY?

On the inside of each invitation write:

Owl I know is that Pooh,
Rabbit, Piglet, and I are
planning a picnic for
(your child's name)

Come to the House at Pooh Corner
(your address)

on (date) *at* (time)

RSVP: (your phone number)

P.S. Don't bring any bees!

GUESS WHOO'S HAVING A BIRTHDAY PARTY?

Decorations

Pooh-Style Picnic

Even if you're planning this party indoors, make it feel like a picnic. Set the table with a red checkered tablecloth—or forget the table and spread the cloth right on the floor! Use a picnic basket for a centerpiece and sit a stuffed Pooh Bear on top.

Serve off of Pooh plates: Draw Pooh's nose and eyes on brown paper plates with a nontoxic black marker. Buy extra plates and cut two 2-inch circles for each Pooh plate. Staple "ears" to plates.

Paint "HUNNY POT" on plain white paper cups and fill with honey graham cracker teddy bears. Allow one cup for each child. Make Christopher Robin's kite-tail napkins for place markers: Use a colored marker to write each child's name

3

on a napkin.

Punch a hole in the corner of each napkin and string a 12-inch knotted piece of ribbon through the hole to resemble a kite tail.

Hang pink Piglet balloons over the table. Make these by drawing Piglet's face on balloons (upside down) and taping a pair of pink construction paper ears on each one. Hang from ceiling, trees, banisters. . . .

Preparation time: 1 hour 15 minutes

Get-Acquainted Activity

Baby Roo Jelly-Bean Bags

Children fill their own bags with jelly beans that they select themselves. The bags will be used in the Roo Toss game, and afterward, the jelly beans will make for fun snacking.

Fig. 1

Materials:

12 beige (or brown) boy's socks
    (light-gauge knit)
4 dozen cotton balls
4 yards heavy-gauge red yarn
scissors
12 white paper sales tags with holes
    (available at stationery supply
    stores)
black felt-tip fabric marker
4 pounds jelly beans, in assorted flavors
Yield: 12 beanbags

Fig. 2

4

Directions:

1. Put about four cotton balls in the toes of each sock and tie off tightly with the red yarn (fig. 1).
2. Thread the sales tags onto the yarn and tie the yarn in a bow. The tied-off portion of the sock will form Roo's head.
3. Draw baby kangaroo faces on heads with a felt-tip fabric marker and write one child's name on each tag.
4. Set up a table with bowls of jelly beans —each flavor in a separate bowl—and a basket of the Baby Roos.

As guests arrive, show them to the table and tell them to fill their own personal Roo with their favorite flavors of jelly beans. When the socks are pretty well stuffed, help the children tightly tie the bottoms closed with more red yarn (fig. 2).
Preparation time: 8 minutes per Roo

Fantasy Feature

Pooh Pals Party Hats

Piglet's ears are just a variation of Eeyore's—for extra fun, make both!

Materials:

EEYORE'S EARS PATTERN (page 7)
2¹/₂ yards 60" wide gray felt (or pink felt for Piglet Ears)
¹/₂ yard 60"-wide pink felt (omit for Piglet Ears)
tracing paper
pencil
tailor's chalk
scissors
fabric glue
stapler
Yield: 12 hats (each pattern)

EEYORE EARS:

1. Trace pattern for ears on tracing paper.
2. Place outer ear pattern on gray felt and mark twenty-four ears with tailor's chalk.
3. Place inner ear pattern on pink felt and mark twenty-four ears with tailor's chalk.
4. Cut out gray and pink ears along lines.
5. Glue pink inner ear on to gray outer ear pieces.
6. Cut twelve 2-inch wide and 22-inch long strips from remaining gray felt for headbands.
7. Use your child's head as a guide to adjust fit of headband.
8. Glue in place and secure with staples. There will be some overlap.
9. Fold each ear (fig. 1) and staple a pair to the inside of headband (fig. 2). The ears

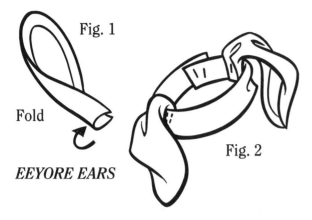

Fig. 1

Fold

EEYORE EARS

Fig. 2

Fold

PIGLET EARS

should drop over the top of headband, with pink inner ears facing forward.

PIGLET EARS
Substitute 2½ yards of pink felt for gray felt. (Omit 1 yard of the pink felt for inner ears.) Trace pattern for PIGLET EARS. Follow method for EEYORE EARS, omitting step for inner ears.
Preparation Time: 1 hour 15 minutes

Games

Hide the Honey from the Heffalumps

In this game, Pooh tries to hide his honey from the heffalumps. Pooh's honey is kept—where else?—in one of those bear-shaped clear plastic bottles filled with honey. (For the purposes of this game, an empty bottle will work best—no sticky accidents!)

One child is Pooh, and all the others are heffalumps. The heffalumps turn their backs and hide their heads in their trunks—that is, under their arms. Meanwhile, Pooh searches the yard or house for a good hiding place. When he's ready, he yells, "Oh, bother. I'm all out of honey." The heffalumps search for the honey. The one who finds it becomes Pooh, and Pooh becomes a heffalump. The cycle continues until most of the players have had a chance to hide the honey.

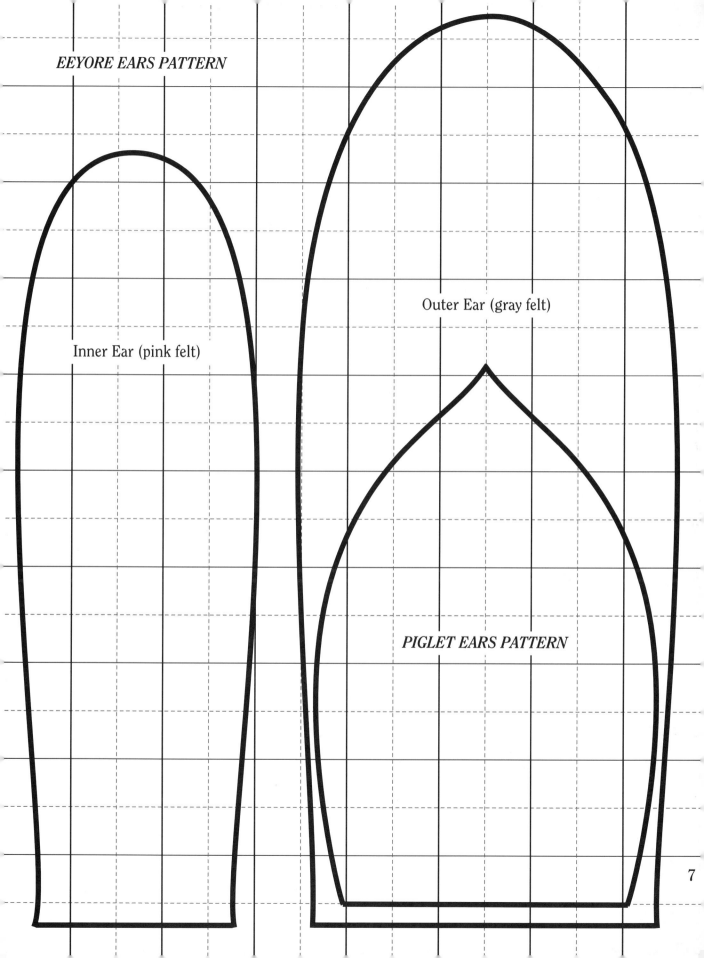

EEYORE EARS PATTERN

Inner Ear (pink felt)

Outer Ear (gray felt)

PIGLET EARS PATTERN

7

Tigger Tag

With his springy tail, Tigger bounces through life. In Tigger Tag, everyone gets to bounce like Tigger.

One child is designated Tigger or "it." All of the children hop around, and Tigger hops after them. When Tigger touches a player, that person must sit down right where he or she was tagged. When the last player left bouncing is tagged, the round is over, and this player becomes Tigger for the next round. The game continues until everyone is all bounced out.

Roo Toss

As Kanga hopped around the Hundred-Acre Wood, she carried Roo around in her pouch. For this activity, children toss their Baby Roo Jelly-Bean Bags into Kanga's pouch.

Find a large appliance box and draw or paint a kangaroo on it. Cut a hole out of the box where Kanga's pouch would be. Put a pillow inside and in front of the box to cushion the beanbag landing.

Children take turns trying to toss their bags into Kanga's pouch. At the end of three rounds, the child with the most successful tosses is the winner. In case of a tie, you can hold a toss-off. For mishaps, such as spilled jelly beans, have extra jelly beans on hand so children can refill their bags.

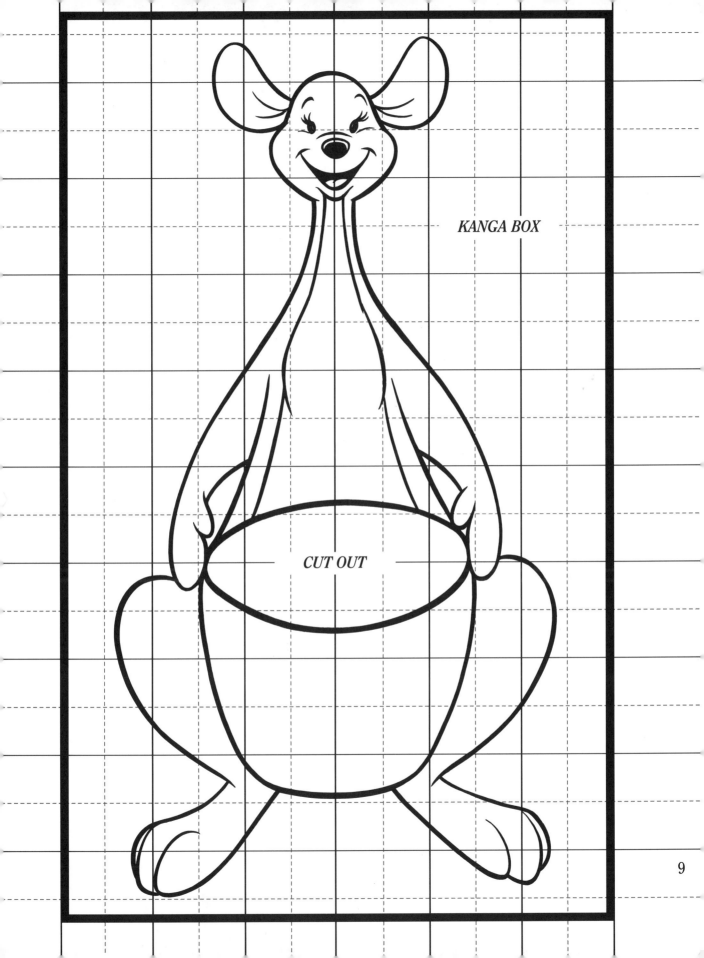

KANGA BOX

CUT OUT

9

101 Dalmatians Puppy Party

Disney's *101 Dalmatians* introduced us to Pongo and Perdita, one of America's favorite couples, as well as the deliciously nasty villainess, Cruella De Vil. I remember first seeing the movie when I was only four years old. Needless to say, it left an impression on me. The next morning I wanted "K-9 Krunchies" for breakfast and decades later . . . I kept all of my dogs' puppies so they could be "one big happy family."

This is a wonderful party for young children. They're fascinated by London's canine culture and De Vil's diabolical plot to kidnap puppies for fur coats. If you're like me, you know families who have worn out their VCR playing *101 Dalmatians* 101 times! From toddlers to their adult escorts, a good time is guaranteed with this theme. The food is fun and the games are engaging.

Invitation

Dalmatian Card

Decorations

Polka-Dot Puppy Motif

Spotted tablecloth, napkins, plates, cups, polka-dot balloons, toy dalmatians, K-9 Krunchies boxes, and personalized dog dish place-markers

Get-Acquainted Activity

Dog Biscuit Bake Shop

Fantasy Feature

Dalmatian Dog Ears and Personalized Dog Collars

Games

The Twilight Bark
Buried Bones
Here Comes Cruella

Menu

Hot Dogs in Bread-Bone Buns......119
K-9 Krunchies......120
Pongo's Pears......121
Chocolate Chip Dog Biscuits......122
Polka-Dot Milk......122
Dalmatian Cake......167
Perdita's Chipper Ice-Cream Pups......194
or Crème De Cruella De Vil......201

Invitation

Dalmatian Card

A smiling polka-dot puppy invites guests to this party at the Dalmatian Plantation, a place just swarming with puppies!

> ### Materials:
>
> *12 (9" x 12") sheets white poster board*
> *4-yard roll ³/4" red plastic tape*
> *12 1¹/2" to 2" gold notary seals*
> *black felt-tip marker*
> *12 (9" x 12") white envelopes*
> *Yield: 12 invitations*

Directions:

1. Cut a 12-inch strip of tape and press it down onto the long side of the poster board, about 2 inches from the bottom (fig. 1).
2. Fold the poster board in half and stick a notary seal in the middle of the tape. This becomes a collar.
3. Draw a dog face on each card, and on the seal write the name of the child to whom the invitation is addressed (fig. 2).
4. Draw spots all over the front and back of the card and on the back of the envelope (fig. 3).
5. Write the following message inside each card:

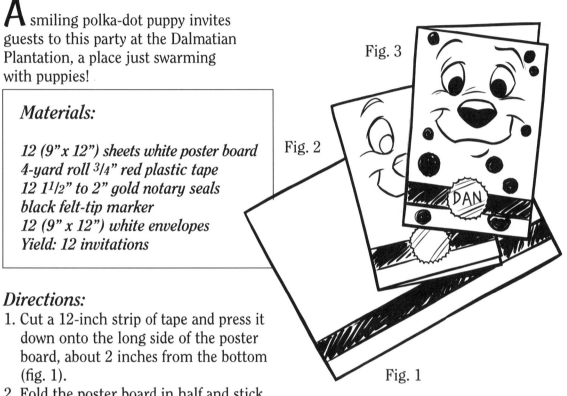

Fig. 3

Fig. 2

Fig. 1

Pongo, Perdita, and (your child's name)
are having a Polka-Dot Puppy Party at the Dalmatian Plantation
(your address)

on (date) *at* (time)

Rooof!SVP: (your phone number)

Preparation time: 1 hour 20 minutes

Decorations

Polka-Dot Puppy Motif

When it comes to dalmatian decorations . . . think dots! Use nontoxic black acrylic paint to sponge spots all over a white paper or plastic tablecloth.

Continue painting polka dots on sturdy white paper (or plastic-coated) plates and cups. You can even cover white balloons with black spots.

If you chose this theme, chances are that you already have some toy Dalmatians around the house. By all means invite them to the party and have them sit at the table! You can also put boxes of K-9 KRUNCHIES (page 120) on the table. Let the kids pour their potato chips or popcorn "kibble" into personalized dog dishes. Simply buy plastic pet bowls and paint each child's name on one. The bowls make great place markers.

Get-Acquainted Activity

Dog Biscuit Bake Shop

12 BISCUITS

Kids love playing with modeling clay—especially when it's edible! For this activity, children mold sugar-cookie dough (studded with chocolate chips) into dog-bone-shaped cookies. Have miniature chips on hand so that cookies can be personalized with each child's name. Be sure to use the shortbread-style cookie dough, see CHOCOLATE CHIP DOG BISCUITS (page 122). If you use packaged cookie dough, the eggs in the dough will cause the bones to expand into blobs!

When guests arrive, bring each child to the table that's set up for the Dog Biscuit Bake Shop. Place a ball of dough in the center of a paper plate, and let each child mold it into a dog-bone shape. Set out a dish of miniature chips for children to spell out their names on their cookies. (Very small children will need help from an adult.) Bake cookies while kids are playing games or eating.

Fantasy Feature

Dalmatian Dog Ears and Personalized Dog Collars

Little kids love to pretend that they're animals. (I know this firsthand . . . take it from someone who wore a "tail" to preschool!) Donning Dalmatian ears and dog collars really puts party guests in the mood for make-believe.

DALMATIAN DOG EARS:

Materials:
Dalmatian Dog Ears Patterns (page 16)

2 yards 60"-wide white felt
*   tracing paper*
pencil
tailor's chalk
scissors
black fabric paint
sponge
fabric glue
stapler
Yield: 12 hats

Directions:

1. Trace pattern for ears on tracing paper.
2. Place pattern on felt and mark twenty-four ears with tailor's chalk. Cut out ears along lines.
3. Cut twelve 2-inch-wide and 24-inch long strips from remaining felt. Use your child's head as a guide to adjust fit of headband.
4. Glue in place and secure with staples (fig. 1). There will be some overlap.
5. Fold each ear (fig. 2) and staple a pair to the inside of each headband. The ears should droop over the top of headband.
6. Dip tip of sponge in black paint and dot the ears and headband to look like Dalmatian spots (fig. 3).

Preparation time: 1¹/₄ hours
Drying time: 6 hours

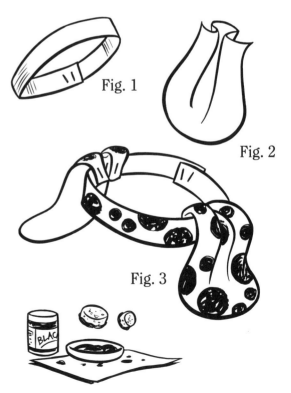

Fig. 1

Fig. 2

Fig. 3

PERSONALIZED DOG COLLARS:

> ### Materials:
>
> *5 yards 1" red grosgrain ribbon*
> *12 jumbo paper clips (brass plated*
> *or red plastic coated)*
> *24 1 1/2–2" self-adhesive gold notary seals*
> *paper hole punch*
> *scissors*
> *black felt-tip permanent ink laundry pen*
> *stapler*
> *Yield: 12 collars*

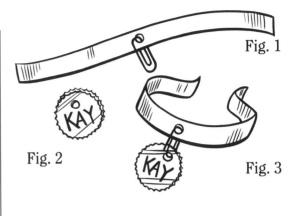

Fig. 1

Fig. 2

Fig. 3

Directions:

1. Cut twelve 15-inch strips of ribbon.
2. Punch a hole in the center of each strip.
3. Hook a paper clip through the hole (fig. 1), then stick two gold seals back-to-back so that you have twelve gold dog tags.
4. Punch holes in the top of the tags and write one child's name on each tag (fig. 2).
5. Hook the tags onto the paper clips (fig. 3).
6. When the children arrive, staple collars around each child's neck, making sure they fit loosely and comfortably.

Preparation time: 45 minutes

Games

The Twilight Bark

From Danny the Great Dane to Old Towser to the Colonel and Sergeant Tibbs, the "Twilight Bark" was like a telegraph. Each dog barked word of the missing puppies clear down the river Thames (although sometimes the message got a little muddled, much the way it does in the game "telephone").

Line up the children across the yard (or large room), about four feet apart from each other. The child at the beginning of the line thinks of a message, runs up to the next child, and whispers it in his or her ear. For very young children, a short message is challenging enough. Slightly older players can use longer messages. The message is passed down the line to the final child, who announces it aloud. Children will enjoy hearing how the message got changed along the way. The player at the end of the line moves to the front of the line and starts a new message. The Twilight Bark continues until each child gets a chance to send his or her own message.

DALMATIAN DOG EARS PATTERN

Buried Bones

Essentially an Easter egg hunt, this game is played using dog biscuits instead of eggs. Buy a large box of multicolored dog biscuits (red, green, and brown). Hide them in secret places around the yard or house. Use an equal amount of each color. Divide the children into three teams: the red team, the green team, and the brown team. Each team goes in search of its bones. A bone in the team color is worth three points. A bone in another team's color is worth only one point. After all of the bones have been accounted for (or a reasonable period of time has elapsed), a tally is taken. The team scoring the most points wins.

Here Comes Cruella

This is essentially a hide-and-seek game. The hiders are Dalmatians and the seeker is Cruella De Vil. (To add to the fun, let Cruella wear a spotted faux fur coat. Just use black fabric paint to cover a white bathrobe or sheet with dots.)

The Dalmatians run and hide in places throughout the house or yard while Cruella sits in her "mansion" (any designated spot) and counts to 101. (Younger children can just count to 10, then add "101" for the effect.)

As soon as the magic number is announced, Cruella calls out "HERE COMES CRUELLA!" and begins her hunt. As soon as Cruella finds a Dalmatian, she takes it back to her mansion. The last Dalmatian to be captured gets to put on the "Dalmatian coat" and play Cruella in the next round. (It's really no surprise that kids consider it a prize to be offered the role of villain in this game.)

The Lion King Party

___ Age 3 to 6 ___

Set amid the majestic African Serengeti, *The Lion King* is visually a feast for parents and a source of wonder for children. In the opening ceremony Mufasa and Sarabi stand on a cliff high atop Pride Rock while their loyal subjects wait below. The great mystic Rafiki raises baby Simba over his head for all to see and gives him the blessing of a future king. However, evil Scar and his hyena henchmen plot to change the rightful course of events. With the death of his father, Simba flees from grief and guilt, taking refuge in the jungle until he comes of age. Meanwhile Scar disrupts the harmony of nature and runs the kingdom into near ruin. In a triumphant return, the mature Simba overthrows his uncle and takes his rightful place on Pride Rock with his childhood friend Nala as his queen.

Children really relate to this colorful take on growing up and becoming part of "the great circle of life." And at a themed party they'll love putting on lions' manes and acting out the parts of all the African animals.

The Lion King Party

Invitation

African Acacia Tree

Decorations

Serengeti Motif

African stuffed animals (lions, elephants, zebras, giraffes . . .), lion paw print tablecloth, zebra cups, grass mats, Little Simba Lion King Cake, Orange Elephants, bonzai tree, safari posters

Get-Acquainted Activity

Personalized Pride Rocks

Fantasy Feature

Mufasa Manes

Games

Circle of Life
Worm-Eating Contest
The Elephant Graveyard

Menu

Wildebeest Burgers with Serengeti Sauce......123
Pride Rock Potatoes......124
Orange Elephants......124
Pumbaa Punch......125
Little Simba Lion King Cake......176
Lion King Ice-Cream Scars......202

Invitation

African Acacia Tree

The *Lion King* opens with a sweeping scene of the Serengeti. Spreading like broad umbrellas are dramatic silhouettes of the flat-topped acacia trees that symbolize the African landscape. This invitation uses the unusual acacia to announce *"A Serengeti Celebration of the Great Circle of Life."*

It's a fun invitation to make with young children. You can draw the trunk of the tree with brown crayons. Your child can help sponge in the foliage and grass. If you don't feel like hand lettering each invitation, simply photocopy the message and glue it under the flap.

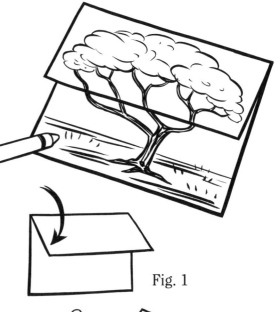

Fig. 1

Fig. 2

Materials:

12 (9" x 12") light blue construction paper
dark and light brown crayons
green tempera paint
pieces of natural sponge
pie tin
12 photocopied messages (instructions follow)
glue or rubber cement
12 (9" x 12") envelopes
Yield: 12 invitations

Directions:

1. Fold the top third of paper down, 4 inches, and crease along top (fig. 1).
2. With dark brown crayon draw trunk of tree and limbs, extending slightly onto the flap.
3. Draw lines for bark inside outlines of trunk and limbs (fig. 2).
4. Use light brown crayon to fill in trunk and limbs and draw blades of grass.
5. Dip a piece of sponge into paint and pat in the top of tree on folded flap. Also use sponge and green paint to fill in around grass, to give the ground some dimension.
6. When paint has dried on invitations, glue

photocopied message under flap (fig. 3).
Type or write the following message
three times on an 8½" x 11" sheet of
paper. Each message should take up a
third of a page. Make four photocopies.
(This may also be printed by
computer.) Cut messages apart.

Fig. 3

Rafiki calls you to come to Pride Rock for
"A Serengeti Celebration of the Great
Circle of Life" marking the birthday of lion
cub (your child's name)
at (your address)
on (date) *at* (time)
ROAR!SVP: (your phone number)

Preparation time: 1 hour 20 minutes

Decorations

Serengeti Motif

To create the atmosphere of the
Serengeti Savanna, you'll have to hunt
down lots of African stuffed animals (the
toy kind, not the taxidermist type!).
Decorate the table and room with all the
lions, elephants, zebras, and giraffes you
have in your house, then borrow more
from friends and neighbors—or have each
guest bring a lion with them
(tell parents to write their
child's name on the tag).

Paint lion paw prints on a
paper or plastic tablecloth. Use
a black waterproof marker to
make zebra stripes on white
paper cups, and set the table
with grass mats.

Use LITTLE SIMBA LION
KING CAKE (page 176) as the
centerpiece and surround it with a herd
of ORANGE ELEPHANTS (page 124). If
you happen to have (or can borrow) a
bonzai tree, it will look somewhat like a
miniature acacia tree on the table—
especially with a few Lion King figurines
sitting under its shade. Finally, your
local travel agency may be able to provide you with safari posters.

21

Get-Acquainted Activity

Personalized Pride Rocks

Any kind of art activity always gets children instantly involved. For this one you'll need to go to your local garden center and pick out a selection of large, smooth river stones. It's wise to have more than one per child. When given a choice, kids get picky over things like the "perfect rock." Also, some kids might want to make several. (This is especially true of early arrivals.)

Set up an activity table as a "Pride Rock Painting Place." Have enough brushes and assorted colors of acrylic paint for all of the children to use. Paint some sample rocks ahead of time. You can paint animals like lions and zebras and paw prints or just names of the characters. The kids can use their imaginations and decorate them any way they like, adding their own names or initials. (To be realistic, very young guests are more likely to paint "Picasso-style" rocks than anything representational. You may want to help them with names or initials.)

Fantasy Feature

Mufasa Manes

Imagine making lion mane hats out of brown paper grocery bags. These are so simple and inexpensive to construct and yet kids are fascinated by them.

The important thing to remember is that you must have the correct size of paper bags. Large grocery bags won't work; neither will the lunch-sack size. Ask your local supermarket if they can supply you with a dozen medium-size bags about 7" x 4 1/2" x 13".

Materials:

12 (8" x 5" x 13") brown paper
*   grocery sacks*
dark brown crayon
scissors
glue
paper clips
4 feet of 1/4" soft elastic
stapler
Yield: 12 hats

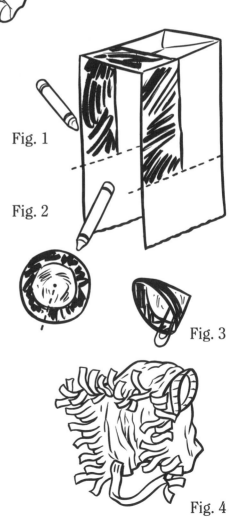

Directions:

1. Trim down bags so that they stand only about eight inches high.
2. Cut out one narrow side of each bag, giving you a 5" x 8" panel. Reserve these panels for ears.
3. With brown crayon, draw a line along the inside of each bag about 3 inches from the cut edge.
4. Remove wrapper from crayon. Use side of crayon to shade paper from the line to the edge (fig. 1).
5. Cut twenty-four 3-inch circles from reserved panels.
6. Shade area inside ear and draw some feathery "fur" around the edges of each circle.
7. Cut a 1-inch slit at the base of each circle (fig. 2). Overlap edges of slit about 1/2 inch and glue to make an ear. Paper clips will help hold glue in place while it dries (fig. 3).
8. Clip through edge of paper bag (the crayon-shaded part) at 1/4-inch to 3/8-inch intervals, creating a fringe. Bend paper backward.
9. Glue ears on each side.
10. Cut 4-inch lengths of elastic and staple at opposite corners at the opening for a chin strap. Scrunch down pointed corners at the back of bag to give a more rounded appearance to the hood (fig. 4).

Fig. 1

Fig. 2

Fig. 3

Fig. 4

Games

Circle of Life

One of the messages from *The Lion King* is that we all have a place in the "great Circle of Life." The life cycle has no beginning or ending. This sort of never-ending version of musical chairs illustrates the principle. The game starts off with a circle of grass or straw place mats. There should be one less mat than the number of players. Play the sound track to *The Lion King* and tell the kids to get down on their hands and knees and pace like lions around the circle of mats.

When the music comes to a halt every "lion" must scramble to sit on the closest mat. Obviously, one lion will be left without a mat. So that lion moves to the other end of the room, and one of the mats from the circle is also removed and placed with the lone lion. The music starts again. This time, while the lions pace around the circle of mats the lone lion paces around his one mat. The process continues (like musical chairs), only each time a lion and a mat are removed from the main circle, they're added to the new circle on the other end of the room. Eventually, the main circle dwindles down to two lions competing for one mat, while all the lions in the new circle have an equal number of mats and lions. At the end of the game, the last lion ends up over at the other circle . . . and guess what? The new circle now has one too many lions for mats and the whole thing starts over again.

Worm-Eating Contest

Simba thought Pumbaa ate some pretty disgusting stuff: grubs, ants, and worms. But, as Pumbaa showed him, it's just an acquired taste that's easily cultivated if you're really hungry. Of course, kids have a hearty appetite for candy gummy worms. This is just a contest to see who can gobble them down the fastest!

For this game, line the kids up, side by side. Tell them that they're warthogs and to get down on their hands and knees. Now for the fun part: Put raisins (ants) and gummy candy worms on a paper plate in front of each player. (All players should have the same number of ants and worms.) At the signal "hakuna matata," the eating begins! (Because warthogs don't have hands, be sure to warn players not to use their fingers, or they'll be disqualified.) The first one to finish is the prize-winning pig!

The Elephant Graveyard

Scar enticed Simba to explore the eerie elephant graveyard by saying, "Only the bravest lions go there." Of course, with that comment, Simba and Nala were off in search of the mysterious Shadow Lands.

The elephant graveyard is a spooky place filled with elephant bones and tusks. Lion cubs beware . . . hungry hyenas lurk there.

For this game, three children are selected to be hyenas: Bazai, Shenzi, and Ed. They defend the elephant graveyard, which is actually a large circle filled with bones. (Use "bones" cut from brown paper.) The bones are then placed inside the circle where the three hyenas stand guard. The lion cubs roam around the circle, waiting for an opportunity to venture inside the circle and carry one of the bones back beyond the border. If a hyena tags them, the lion cub must switch places with the hyena, and the bone is placed on that spot. The new lion cub has to go back outside the border with the other cubs. (Cubs that were just hyenas can't carry a bone out with them!) The goal of the game is for the lion cubs to get all of the bones outside of the circle. If this is played outdoors, the circle can be very large. If played indoors, the circle will be smaller. It's more challenging, in that case, to have both the lion cubs and hyenas crawl around on hands and knees.

Peter Pan Party

Age 5 to 8

Wendy Darling entertains her brothers, John and Michael, with tales about Peter Pan, an adventure-loving boy who lives in Never Land and refuses to grow up. To Wendy's father Peter Pan is nonsensical make-believe, but to Wendy and the boys he is very real. One night, Wendy's father forbids her to tell any more Peter Pan stories. That very night, while Wendy's parents are out, Peter Pan appears at the Darling household to retrieve the shadow he has left behind! Peter teaches the three children to fly, and with the fairy Tinker Bell, leads them off to Never Land, where they meet the Lost Boys, Tiger Lily, and the wicked Captain Hook.

The timeless quality of Peter Pan appeals to us all, especially little boys who want to be pirates! Ask any six-year-old who ever swashbuckled with an imaginary sword or wore an eye patch on Halloween. Just thinking about this party makes me wish I'd never grown up.

Peter Pan Party

Invitation
Map to Never Land

Decorations
Never Land Motif
Color-in map of Never Land tablecloth, Crocodile Coin Clips, Crocodile Cake,
teepee napkins, pirate-ship sails, skull-and-crossbones flag,
kitchen timer for clock sound effects

Get-Acquainted Activity
Peter Pan and Pirate Party Hats

Fantasy Feature
Crocodile Coin Clips

Games
Peter Pan's Shadow Hunt
Walk the Plank
Captain Hook's Treasure Chest

Menu
Pirate Ship Poor Boys......126
Tiger Lily's Totem Pole Potatoes......127
Tinkerbell's Tangerine Punch......127
Crocodile Cake......168
Captain Hook Ice-Cream Heads......203

Invitation

Map to Never Land

The invitation for the Peter Pan party comes with a map to Never Land—and pixie dust for flying there! Simply draw the map on a sheet of typing paper and make twelve copies.

Materials:
black felt-tip marker
2 sheets typing paper
crayons
gold or silver glitter
12 letter-size mailing envelopes
Yield: 12 invitations

Directions:

1. Begin by drawing a map of Never Land (next page) on the first sheet of paper with a black felt-tip marker. Be sure to include Pirate's Cove, Crocodile Creek, Mermaid Lagoon, Skull Rock, Indian Camp, Misty Mountains, the Sea of Imagination, and Hangman's Tree.
2. On the second sheet of paper, write the following message:

> *This is your pass to a Peter Pan Birthday Party*
> *Sprinkle this pixie dust over your head on* (date), *and fly to Never Land!*
> *At* (time) *knock three times on Hangman's Tree at* (your address) *and ask for* (your child's name)
> *RSVP:* (your phone number)

3. Make copies so that the map is on one side and the message is on the other side of the same sheet of paper.
4. Use crayons to color each map.
5. Fold the invitations, letter style, placing a teaspoon of glitter—Tinker Bell's pixie dust—in each one. Slip into envelopes and mail.

Decorations

Never Land Motif

The decor for a Peter Pan party can be as eclectic as Never Land itself. From Pirate's Cove and the Indian Camp to Skull Rock and Hangman's Tree, there's certainly a wealth of possibilities! One way to incorporate all these themes is to use a map (like the one on the invitation) as a tablecloth. Draw Never Land on a

NEVER LAND

SKULL ROCK

MERMAID LAGOON

SEA OF IMAGINATION

MISTY MOUNTAINS

CROCODILE CREEK

HANGMAN'S TREE

INDIAN CAMP

PIRATE'S COVE

large white paper tablecloth. Fill in the ocean (the Sea of Imagination) with blue crayon. Set out crayons on the table so that the children can color in the rest of the map. CROCODILE COIN CLIPS (next page) can mark place settings, and the CROCODILE CAKE (page 168) serves as the centerpiece. Fold paper napkins to look like Native American teepees, and decorate them with crayons.

You can even rig pirate-ship sails across the ceiling (or from a clothesline) using white sheets. And, of course, you've just got to make a black flag with a white skull and crossbones.

Finally, add some sound effects for atmosphere. Remember how Captain Hook's old enemy, the Crocodile, swallowed a clock! Find a noisy windup clock or kitchen timer, and hide it somewhere close by.

Get-Acquainted Activity

Peter Pan and Pirate Party Hats

Peter Pan is dressed in green, from his pixie-pointed boots to his jaunty cap—except for the splash of red at the very top. Children can get into the Never Land spirit by making their own paper Peter Pan hats with bright red plumes. Substitute black tissue paper and you have classic pirate hats. Why not offer a choice?

Fig. 6

Materials:

12 (20" x 30") sheets green tissue paper*
stapler
12 red feathers (sold by the bag at craft and hobby shops). If these aren't readily available, cut "feathers" out of red construction paper.
Yield: 12 hats

Make up a sample hat, and set it on a craft table along with the paper, stapler, and feathers. As each child arrives, show him or her how to make the hat.

1. First fold a sheet of tissue paper into a 20" x 15" rectangle, then into a 10" x 15" rectangle, with the main fold at the top (figs. 1 and 2).

30

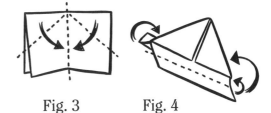

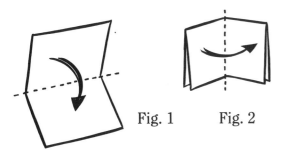

Fig. 1   Fig. 2   Fig. 3   Fig. 4

2. Fold down the corners of the top 7 inches on each side (fig. 3).
3. Fold up the bottom of each side 1 inch and crease.
4. Fold up another inch and crease again (fig. 4).
5. Tuck one end under the other about 1¹/₂ inches on each side, and staple in place (fig. 5).
6. At one end of the hat, behind a fold, staple a red feather in place (fig. 6).

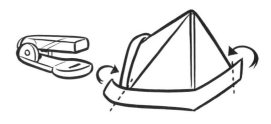

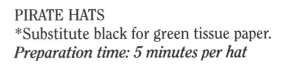

Fig. 5

PIRATE HATS
*Substitute black for green tissue paper.
Preparation time: 5 minutes per hat

Fantasy Feature

Crocodile Coin Clips

The Crocodile Coin Clip is a clothespin contraption that makes a clever money clip, letter holder, potato chip bag clip, or even hair barrette. I like to use these crocs as place-card clips, each one grasping a child's name and a gold-foil-covered chocolate coin.

Materials:

12 spring-action wooden clothespins
green felt-tip marker (wide)
black felt-tip marker
2 dozen glue-on hobby eyes, 3/8" diameter
hobby glue (clear drying, super hold)
1 (9"x 12") sheet green construction paper
scissors
pencil
ruler
12 gold-foil-covered chocolate coins
Yield: 12 clips

Directions:

1. With the green felt-tip marker, color the entire exterior surface of the clothespins. (It's not necessary to color inside the mouth.)
2. Glue an eye on each side of the pin, behind the large circular opening.
3. With the black felt-tip pen, make two dots at the nose end of clothespin for nostrils.
4. Cut the green paper into twelve 3-inch square cards.
5. Along the bottom of each card, write the name of one guest and clip it, with a gold coin, between the jaws of a crocodile. Use as place markers.

Preparation time: 30 minutes

Games

Peter Pan's Shadow Hunt

Peter Pan first met Wendy and her brothers when he visited the nursery in search of his missing shadow. Wendy's first act of friendship was to sew Peter's shadow back on for him.

For this game you'll need twelve sheets of black tissue paper. Cut the silhouette figure of a boy out of one sheet. Crumple it into a wad. Crumple the other eleven sheets of tissue paper as well. Hide all twelve sheets in various places around the house or yard. Children must go in search of the shadow, and the one who brings it back is the winner.

Walk the Plank

Captain Hook's band of pirates hid near Hangman's Tree in hopes of capturing Peter Pan. Instead, they kidnapped Wendy, Michael, John, and the Lost Boys and brought them all back to Hook's ship. There Captain Hook ordered his prisoners to join the crew . . . or walk the plank!

This game is basically a balance test.

the ground. (The plank should stand only about 2 to 3 inches above the ground.) Children pretend that they are Captain Hook's captives and line up at one end of the plank. Pass out twelve wide, loose-fitting rubber bands for the children to bind their wrists together behind their backs. The players take turns walking across the plank, trying not to lose their balance and step off. As each child finishes, he or she goes back to the end of the line for another round. Any player who doesn't make it across is "eaten by the crocodile"—in other words, is out. Eventually, almost everyone will end up overboard. The last remaining player is the prize-winning plank walker.

You'll need a sturdy, straight 6-foot-long two-by-four for a plank and two bricks or concrete blocks. Prop the board up at each end with a brick so that the 4-inch side is parallel to

Captain Hook's Treasure Chest

Fishing for favors is a time-honored party activity. Usually it's done with fishing rods. This game is a slight variation on the theme. First you'll need to make a treasure chest by decorating a large cardboard box. (If you already have some kind of trunk, so much the better!) Fill the chest with candy and/or favors that have been wrapped in colored tissue with a ribbon loop on each. For Captain Hook's hook use a coat hanger. Bend the hanger so that there's a handle for holding the hook.

Kids take turns being blindfolded and reaching into the chest with the hook to get a prize. If the hook snares more than one favor, the extra favors must be thrown back.

The Little Mermaid Party

── Age 4 to 8 ──

Ariel lives under the sea along with a host of colorful characters, including her father, King Triton; her best friend, Flounder; and Sebastian, the singing crab. But the Little Mermaid longs to be part of the human world. One night she spots the handsome human Prince Eric, and it's love at first sight. In order to win his heart, Ariel enlists the help of Ursula, the evil Sea Witch. (But Ursula has a wicked plan to snare Eric for herself!) In the end, it's Prince Eric to the rescue, and in gratitude King Triton grants his daughter her dearest wish: to become human and marry her prince.

This is such a popular theme with little girls. The Little Mermaid makes a wonderful backyard party in warm weather. Ask the kids to wear swimsuits and expect everyone to get really wet and sandy!

Invitation

Scallop Shell

Decorations

Caribbean Sea Motif

Seashells, coral, fishnets, fishbowl with live goldfish

Get-Acquainted Activity

King Triton's Shell Shop

Fantasy Feature

Ariel's Treasure Chest

with dinglehoppers & bubble-blowing snarfblatts

Games

Starfish Fishing

Sand Castle Contest

March of the Mermaids

Menu

Under the Sea Biscuits......128

Fruity Flounders......129

Guppy Cups......129

Caribbean Blue Cooler......130

Sebastian's Crab Cakes......179

Ursula's Icy Sea Witches......204

Invitation

Scallop Shell

Marbleized wrapping paper in pastel shades makes a lovely cover for this invitation. You can also use rainbow cellophane that has a luminous quality similar to a seashell.

Fig. 1

Fig. 2

Materials:

13 (9" x 12") sheets white
   poster board
tracing paper
glue or rubber cement
1 package or roll
   pearlized cellophane or
   marbleized wrapping paper
4 yards pastel or iridescent
   pearlized ribbon
scissors
pencils
pink felt-tip marker
stapler
12 (9" x 12") white
   envelopes
Yield: 12 invitations

Directions:

1. With tracing paper and pencil, trace the scallop shell pattern on next page.
2. Cut out the tracing and glue it to one sheet of the poster board.
3. Cut this out and use it as a stencil for cutting twelve shells each from the poster board and from the gift wrap.
4. Decorate the poster board along its edges with pink marker to form a border (fig. 1).
5. In the center of each poster board shell, write the following message:

> **Ariel invites you under the sea**
> **to a party among the Merpeople for**
> (your child's name)**'s birthday**
> **on** (date) **at** (time)
> (your address)
> **RSVP:** (your phone number)

6. Cut ribbon into 12-inch lengths.
7. Anchor both the ribbon (at its center) and wrapping paper shells to the poster board at base of shell, using a stapler.
8. Knot ribbon once around staple and tie a bow (fig. 2). If using a curling ribbon, gently curl ends. Mail in oversize envelopes.

Preparation time: 1¹/₄ hours

SCALLOP SHELL INVITATION

37

Decorations

Caribbean Sea Motif

Any party shop or import store that carries luau (or island) paraphernalia is the right place to go for mermaid supplies. The party room should have seashells, coral branches, and so forth—and, of course, a fishnet over a blue (or green) paper tablecloth. You can also use shells you've collected as vacation souvenirs or borrow them from friends. For a centerpiece, how about a goldfish bowl with blue gravel and a castle? Add a real goldfish, and you can use it as the grand prize for starfish fishing contest. Be sure to have a Chinese food-type take-out carton lined with a plastic bag, for the winner to take the fish home.

Get-Acquainted Activity

King Triton's Shell Shop

As guests begin arriving, gather them together in King Triton's Shell Shop. This can be a room, screen porch, or a table outside. While the kids mingle with each other, they can decorate seashells with sets of pastel felt-tipped markers. Surprise! You can collect these shells at your local super-market. Just look for boxes of jumbo shells in the pasta isle. These make fun additions to Ariel's Treasure Chest (below).

Fantasy Feature

Ariel's Treasure Chest

Ariel kept many of her precious treasures gathered from sunken ships in a huge treasure chest, hidden away in her secret cave. Among her most prized possessions were a dinglehopper and a snarf-blatt! If you don't have a dozen empty shoe boxes at your house, take up a collection around the neighborhood.

Materials:

12 shoe boxes
aluminum foil
brown spray paint
8 yards gold cord or ribbon
scissors
12 gold notary seals
12 sheets gold cellophane
12 plastic bubble pipes
12 small bottles of bubble solution
12 plastic forks
24 tags (strung with ribbon)
12 bags of gold foil-covered chocolate
    coins
Yield: 12 chests

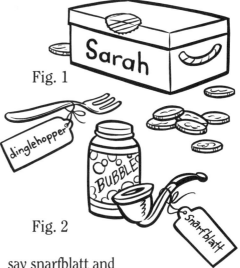

Fig. 1

Fig. 2

Directions:

1. Place boxes and lids, open ends down, on aluminum foil (foil will not stick to the spray-painted materials).
2. Spray boxes and lids, coating thoroughly. Allow to dry for twenty-four hours.
3. Punch two holes, 3" apart, in the center of each of the short sides of the boxes.
4. Cut 6-inch lengths of cord, string them through holes, and knot them on inside of boxes to make handles.
5. Affix a gold notary seal on the center edge of each lid to resemble a latch (fig. 1).
6. Label bubble pipe and fork with tags that say snarfblatt and dinglehopper (fig. 2).
7. Line each box with gold polyester film.
8. Arrange a bubble pipe, bottle of bubbles, and a fork in each box, along with a bag of chocolate coins.
9. Place a box at each child's seat. Children can add their decorated pasta shells and game prizes to this favor box.

Note: Gold glitter paint can be used to write one child's name on each box, allowing the boxes to double as place markers. If you don't want to paint boxes, you can always cover them with brown construction paper.

Preparation time: 1¹/₂ hours
Drying time for paint: 24 hours

Games

Starfish Fishing

In the Starfish Fishing game, children gather around a plastic wading pool and take turns fishing for plastic starfish. (See construction information below for mak-

ing plastic starfish.) Tie magnets to the ends of two fishing poles. (You can use yardsticks tied with string instead of fishing poles.) The starfish are weighted down by steel paper clips, which the magnets will attract. The starfish are numbered 1 through 12 to coordinate with assorted grab-bag prizes (wrapped and numbered 1 through 12). If a child should happen to catch two starfish at once, one of the starfish has to be thrown back into the water. When all of the fish have been caught, it's time to pass out the prizes.

Materials:

6 sheets colored transparent acetate
holepunch
12 jumbo paper clips
waterproof laundry marker
Yield: 12 starfish

Directions:
1. Cut starfish from colored transparent acetate report covers (stars should be about 3 inches across). Punch one hole in a point on each starfish (fig. 1).
2. Clip jumbo paper clips through the holes. Number the starfish 1 through 12, using a waterproof laundry marker (fig. 2).

Note: Paper clips rust, so don't throw starfish in the water-filled wading pool until just before the party starts.

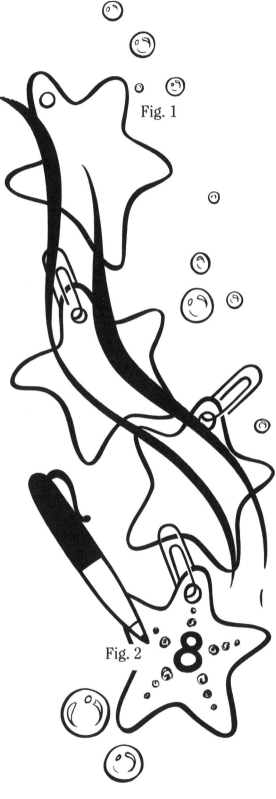

Fig. 1

Fig. 2

40

Sand Castle Contest

This is a game challenging two teams of "builders" in a race against the clock. It can be done in a large sandbox (with teams at opposite ends) or in two small wading pools filled with damp sand. Both teams get identical tools: shovels, buckets, cups, bowls, gelatin molds—anything that can be used to shape sand. Decide on a time limit, according to your party schedule. Then set a kitchen timer for the number of minutes and signal both teams to start. The race is to see which team can build the biggest sand castle in the allotted time. *Note:* Some children prefer to compete on the basis of quality rather than quantity. If the kids decide that the most beautiful castle should win, recruit an impartial third party as judge.

March of the Mermaids

When you were a kid, did you ever try walking around the swimming pool with your flippers on? If you were like me, you did and were probably a constant source of irritation to the lifeguard. Let's face it, wearing webbed feet is fun—even if you do look like a duck. Just imagine how mermaids must feel. . . . That's what this game's all about.

Divide the children into two teams. For each team you'll need a pair of swim fins. (Because kids have different shoe sizes, fins with adjustable straps on the back work best.) Line teams up, parallel to each other. Place a large seashell about 20 feet away, opposite the lineup. The first player in each line straps on a pair of fins. At the starting signal, they must walk around the shell and back to the line, where they take off the fins and pass them to the next player up. The relay continues. *Note:* This should be done on a grassy yard or sandy beach. Do not actually walk around a swimming pool, concrete, asphalt, or tile surface. Mermaids can sometimes stumble with webbed feet (that's part of the fun) but you want a cushion of soft ground or sand.

Cinderella's Ball

—— Age 4 to 8 ——

Cinderella is the romantic story of a girl who is mistreated by her cruel stepmother and stepsisters. On the night of the royal ball, Cinderella's Fairy Godmother transforms her out of her rags and into a vision of beauty just in time to meet Prince Charming. At the stroke of midnight, when Cinderella has to run off and leave the prince, she accidentally leaves behind a glass slipper. The king orders the grand duke to search for the slipper's owner, and when he matches it to Cinderella's foot, Cinderella and the prince are reunited forever.

This is perhaps the most famous fairy tale of all time. Disney's *Cinderella* is such a beloved classic that mothers still ask me about throwing Cinderella parties as if the movie were a new release. The theme also makes a whimsical Halloween party. You can invite guests to come dressed as members of the royal court. October is the perfect time of year to decorate the table with a pumpkin coach and serve frosty ice-cream pumpkins.

Invitation

See-Through Slipper

Decorations

Castle Motif

Balloon ballroom chandelier, herald with kazoo trumpet, red wrapping-paper carpet, paper lace tablecloth, "fine china" paper plates, Golden Tiaras, Classic Disney Castle Cake, Glass Slipper Soda, pumpkin coach

Get-Acquainted Activity

Candy Crown Jewels

Fantasy Feature

Golden Tiaras

Games

Dress-Up Dash
The Cinder Sweep
Cinderella's Designer Gown

Menu

Princess Pasta......130
or Royal Coach Wheels Primavera......131
Breadstick Brooms......132
Glass Slipper Soda......133
Classic Disney Castle Cake......188
Frosty Pumpkins......206
or Disney Ice-Cream Dream Castle......207

Invitation

See-Through Slipper

A slip of a shoe you can see right through, and it slides right into an envelope! The invitation is made out of a transparent piece of plastic acetate.

Directions:
1. With tracing paper and pencil, trace the shoe pattern (next page).
2. Cut the tracing out, and use as a pattern to cut a slipper out of each acetate sheet.
3. Outline the edges of each slipper with glitter paint, and write the following message on each one:
   Princess (guest's name)*'s*
   presence is requested
   at the grand ballroom
   of (your child's name)*'s palace*
   for a royal birthday party
   (your address)
   on (date) *at* (time)
   RSVP on royal phone line
   (your phone number)
Preparation time: 1¹/₄ hours

Materials:

12 (8¹/₂" x 11") sheets clear plastic acetate or 6 clear report covers, split in half along fold
tracing paper
pencil
glue or rubber cement
1 tube silver glitter paint (squeezable)
black felt-tip marker (permanent ink laundry marker)
12 (9" x 12") white envelopes
12 gold notary seals
gold ink pen
scissors
Yield: 12 invitations

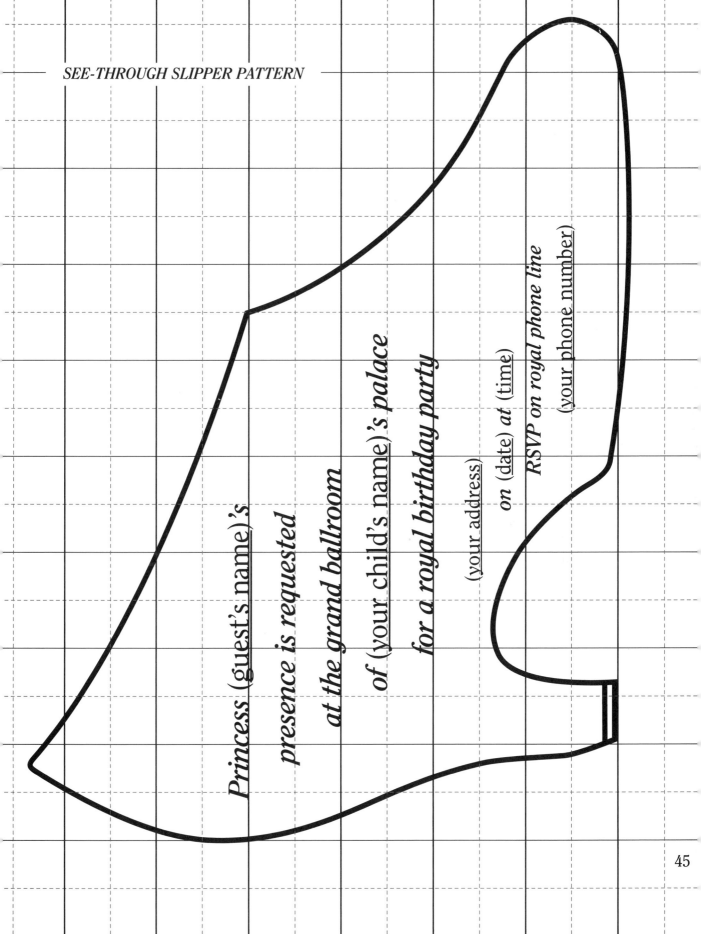

SEE-THROUGH SLIPPER PATTERN

Princess (guest's name)'s

presence is requested

at the grand ballroom

of (your child's name)'s palace

for a royal birthday party

(your address)

on (date) at (time)

RSVP on royal phone line

(your phone number)

Decorations

Castle Motif

Your home is your castle . . . but for this party, it becomes the Crown Prince's palace. For an opulent touch, try making a tiered chandelier from balloons. Use oblong white or silvery balloons and hang them in a bouquet from the ceiling. Add strips of rainbow cellophane and streamers of rainbow ribbon for the shimmering effect of crystal. Appoint a royal officer at the door to announce the entrance of each visiting princess—fanfare from a kazoo trumpet gives it an official touch! You can even roll out the red carpet with a roll of red wrapping paper.

Set the table with a paper lace tablecloth. Decorate paper plates with gold felt-tip markers around the rims, imitating fine china. Display fantasy-feature tiaras on each plate. CLASSIC DISNEY CASTLE CAKE (page 188) takes its place of prominence as the centerpiece. At one end serve GLASS SLIPPER SODA (page 133) from a punch bowl. At the other end decorate a pumpkin with paper coach wheels (if in season).

Get-Acquainted Activity

Candy Crown Jewels

For the opening activity, spearmint sapphires, raspberry rubies, and edible emeralds are laced on licorice necklaces. After each princess makes her entrance to your child's party, escort her to the crown jeweler. This is a table set up with bowls of every kind of candy with holes (hard candies, fruit gels, etc.) and even donut-shaped cereal. Guests thread their own necklaces or bracelets on long strings of red licorice and then knot the ends together.

Fantasy Feature

Golden Tiaras

Look for gold foil at your local florist or party supply store.

Materials:

12 (¹/₂" to ³/₄"-wide) plastic head-bands
6 yards 30"-wide gold florist foil
glue
scissors
large colored sequins
Yield: 12 tiaras

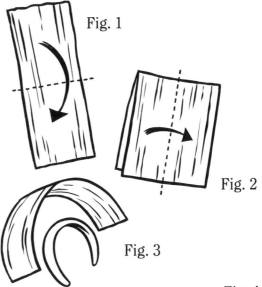

Fig. 1

Fig. 2

Fig. 3

Fig. 4

Directions:

1. Cut the foil into ¹/₂-yard lengths so that you have twelve 18" x 30" pieces.
2. For each tiara, fold the foil in half, into an 18" x 15" rectangle (fig. 1).
3. Fold it in half again, into a 9" x 15" rectangle (fig. 2), and mold it around the contours of the headband (fig. 3). There should be about 8 inches of foil extending from the headband.
4. Pinch the foil at intervals to create a scalloped effect.
5. Twist excess foil back at the ends and glue sequins across the headband (fig. 4).

Preparation time: 1 hour

Games

Dress-Up Dash

On the night of the royal ball, Cinderella was always in a hurry. First she had to rush to reach the palace, and then she had to run home early—leaving her legendary slipper behind.

For this dress-up race, you'll need two suitcases with similar apparel: an oversize dress or jacket (for the girls to pull on over their clothing), a hat, some jewelry, and facsimiles of a glass slipper. (You can use a pair of clear plastic beach sandals and put one sandal in each suitcase.) Players are divided into two teams and line up across the room from the suitcases. The first player on each team is given a magic wand. (See SLEEPING BEAUTY'S DISNEY PRINCESS PIZZA PARTY, Fantasy Feature, page 95.) At the sound of twelve chimes (or bongs on a pan), the race begins. Two players rush to the suitcases, each one taps it with her wand, opens it, and puts on everything in the suitcase. The players then take everything off, put the clothing back in the suitcase, close it, pick up the wand, and rush back to tag the next player on their team. (Each player must first be tapped on the head by the wand before taking it for the next round.) The first team to finish wins the title Best Dressed.

The Cinder Sweep

In this game, colored confetti cinders are swept into the opposing team's territory to score a goal. You'll need about eight cups of colored confetti, twelve brooms—you may want to ask guests to bring their own when they RSVP—and two folding fireplace or makeshift screens.

Set up the game in a large unfurnished area with a smooth floor (no carpeting). Stand a screen at each end of the room and pour confetti in a line across the center of the room. Divide the players into two teams. Each team appoints offensive and defensive players. Offensive players line up at the center line, and defensive players guard their

48

screen. At a signal, the match begins. The offensive players try to sweep as much confetti as they can into the opposing team's screen while the defense struggles to sweep incoming confetti out. After five or six minutes, the closing signal sounds and the game comes to an end. The winning team is the one with the most confetti in the other team's area. (If it's a close call, sweep up each team's confetti in a dust pan, and pour it into a glass measuring cup for a final judgment.)

Cinderella's Designer Gown

When Cinderella first received word of the ball, she didn't have a thing to wear. She found an old pink dress left by her mother, but it was much too plain for such a grand party. Alas! She left it up in the attic and went about her dreary chores. But her little friends, the birds and mice, were quite resourceful. They gathered beads, ribbon, lace, and a lovely sash—cast off by Cinderella's stepsisters. With a bit of tailoring, they designed a new dress for Cinderella to wear. (Of course, the stepsisters later recognized their trimmings on Cinderella and ripped up the dress. It was up to Cinderella's Fairy Godmother to whip up a new one.)

In this activity, children pretend that they are the birds and mice. It's up to them to transform an otherwise frumpy frock with odds and ends. If possible, draw a basic gown on a large chalkboard with an easel stand and provide a box of colored chalk. Or, get some butcher's paper and draw a large dress on that and lay it on a hard floor. Crayons and water-based markers are the perfect tools here. Children take turns adding one distinctive feature to the dress. Design by committee frequently results in outrageous fashion . . . but that's what makes it fun. Since this isn't a game, there are no winners or losers. It's over when the dress is done, but don't be surprised if the children want to start another one!

Happy Unbirthday Tea Party

—— Age 4 to 8 ——

Lewis Carroll created *Alice's Adventures in Wonderland* based on the whimsical stories he told to six-year-old Alice Liddell back in 1865. The masterful artists at Disney lived up to this literary legacy when they released the animated version of *Alice in Wonderland*, a classic in its own right.

To me, the most enchanting element of this story is the "unbirthday" party. What a great concept! A birthday comes once a year, but everyone has 364 unbirthdays. Unbirthdays are a real boon to all the summer and Christmas holiday babies. Perhaps you or your child are members of this special club? If so, you know the feeling. Parties during summer vacation have poor attendance records. With December parties, Santa tries to crowd your birthday and Christmas into one convenient gift. Anyway you look at it, you grow up feeling a little bit deprived.

An unbirthday is a great opportunity to celebrate a birthday on the half year, by reversing the dates (if that works mathematically), on the New Year, on the first day of spring, or any other formula you or your child dream up. Another way to look at unbirthdays is as an opportunity to celebrate every day of life. You can throw a party for no particular reason, except for FUN! What about unbirthday presents? You might want to consider asking each child to bring a modest gift, pool the packages together, then redistribute the presents. This way it's everybody's birthday! (With this practice, unbirthdays could become the most popular type to attend.)

Invitation

Mad Hatter's Top Hat

Decorations

Wonderland Motif

Wrong-way signs, Cheshire Cat smiles, lawn flamingos, cardboard cutouts of
enormous household objects, doll furniture, paper lanterns, color in the
roses tablecloth, mismatched chairs and place settings, teapot

Get-Acquainted Activity

Marshmallow Magic Mushroom Factory

Fantasy Feature

Foil Flamingo Beanbag Birds

Games

The Queen of Hearts's House of Cards
Mad Hatter's Hat Rack
Pin the Grin on the Cheshire Cat

Menu

Cheshire Cat Canapés......133
Queen of Hearts Card Canapés......134
Marshmallow Magic Mushrooms......135
Tweedledum and Tweedledee Tea......135
Mad Hatter Madcap Cupcakes......181
Mad Hatter Ice-Cream Heads......195

Invitation

Mad Hatter's Top Hat

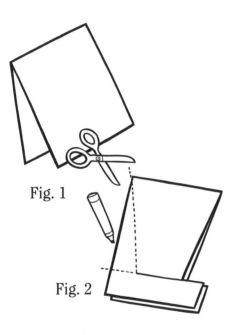

Fig. 1

Fig. 2

Fig. 3

Materials:

*6 (9" x 12") sheets of light green con-
    struction paper*
pencil
scissors
dark green felt-tip marker
12 (3⁵/₈" x 6¹/₂") envelopes
Yield: 12 invitations

Directions:
1. Cut each paper into two 4¹/₂" x 12" strips.
2. Fold in half to make 4¹/₂" x 6" cards,
   with fold at top (fig. 1).
3. Cut cards according to pattern, with the
   top of hat on the fold (do not cut
   through fold) (fig. 2).
4. Draw a 1-inch-wide hatband, about the
   brim of the hat, with marker (fig. 3).
5. Write the following message inside:

> *DON'T BE LATE...*
> *to tea with the*
> *MAD HATTER*
> *to celebrate* <u>(your child's name)</u>*'s*
> *UNBIRTHDAY!*
> *Come to Wonderland* <u>(your address)</u>
> *on* <u>(date)</u> *at* <u>(time)</u>
> *RSVP* <u>(your number)</u>
> *ask for the White Rabbit!*

The tip of a top hat announces this tea
party. Guests are sent a Mad Hatter's hat
card, inviting them to celebrate an
unbirthday.

6. Seal cards in envelopes and mail.
Preparation time: 1 hour

Decorations

Wonderland Motif

The dreamlike, almost disconnected events in *Alice in Wonderland* set the tone for this decor. Every scene from the film can be successfully combined in one party theme. (It's OK to mix the Mad Hatter's tea party with the Queen of Hearts' court of cards.) You can start by decorating outside the house. In search of the White Rabbit, Alice was always lost. Signs weren't much help, since they sent her in every direction! If you have a tree or post at the end of a driveway, make arrows and mark: YONDER, THIS WAY, THAT WAY, ANY WAY, WHICH WAY, WRONG WAY, RIGHT WAY. Post these signs, pointing in all directions (except, of course, for RIGHT WAY, which is the way to your house). You can also put up some Cheshire Cat smiles in trees or bushes. Do you have any pink lawn flamingos? (This fifties fad made a brief comeback in the eighties as a novelty item.) If you are so fortunate, by all means, stick your flamingos out in the yard. When the guests finally get to the front door, tape up a little cardboard door right next to it. (Always too large or too small, doors were a major dilemma for Alice.)

Once inside, you can recreate Wonderland using the undersized, oversized motif. Make cardboard cutouts of enormous household objects in one area, then arrange doll furniture in another. If you remember the tea party scene from the movie, you may recall the Mad Hatter's decorations. He had col-

lapsible paper lanterns in every shape and color strung overhead. You can purchase these from a party shop and do exactly the same. Draw the outlines of red roses all over a white paper tablecloth. Fill the leaves in with green crayon. Cover the table with the cloth and set out small flowerpots of red crayons (for children to "paint the roses red"). In keeping with the Mad Hatter's sense of style, use mismatching chairs, plates, cups, and flatware. If using paper or plastic utensils, you can write **DRINK ME** on the cups and **EAT ME** on the plates. Don't forget to serve the tea (even though it's iced) from a teapot.

Get-Acquainted Activity

Marshmallow Magic Mushroom Factory

In *Alice in Wonderland*, the haughty caterpillar tempted (at that time tiny) Alice into tasting his magic mushroom, if she wished to change her size. Of course, she grew taller than the trees. This activity lets kids make as many of the tasty toadstools as their mouths can handle. They're really quite simple…just vanilla wafers, marshmallows, and melted chocolate.

Prepare the melted chocolate as described in MARSHMALLOW MAGIC MUSHROOMS (page 135). The rest of the ingredients can be set up on a table where kids can work on "mushroom making." Put the vanilla wafers and marshmallows in large bowls. I find that the best (and safest) way to keep chocolate melted at the table is to use an electric coffee cup warmer. These are great because they don't get hot enough to scorch the chocolate or the kids.

Pour melted chocolate into a glass bowl and place on the coffee cup warmer. Show kids how to dip one end of a marshmallow in chocolate and stick the flat bottom on a vanilla wafer on the chocolate to resemble a mushroom cap. (If desired, you can put some cocoa in a sugar shaker to dust the marshmallow stems. This looks like soil.) You might want to make up a sample plate of mushroom prototypes for the kids to get the idea. No doubt these will rapidly disappear!

Fantasy Feature

Foil Flamingo Beanbag Birds

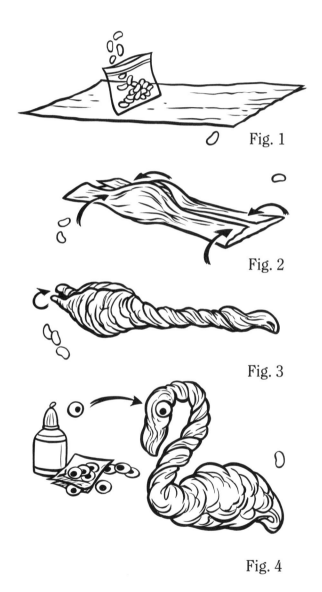

Fig. 1

Fig. 2

Fig. 3

Fig. 4

Preparation time: 5 minutes for each flamingo

Have you ever been to a restaurant where they wrapped your leftovers in a foil swan? Well, this is sort of the same idea. Pink florist foil is used to make long-necked flamingos filled with pink gourmet jelly beans. You can sit these right on the plates at the party table.

Materials:

8 yards pink florist foil
3 pounds gourmet jelly beans (choose pink flavors)
12 zip-style sandwich bags
24 (1/2") movable hobby eyes (glue-on style)
glue
scissors
Yield: 12 beanbag birds

Directions:
For each flamingo:
1. Cut a sheet of foil, 2 feet long.
2. Put about 4 ounces of jelly beans in a sandwich bag and place off center from one end of foil (fig. 1).
3. Fold up end and sides so that only the pink surface of the foil shows (fig. 2).
4. Crimp foil around jelly beans for body and twist for a long neck (fig. 3).
5. Bend and shape neck, beak, and a slight tail. Glue hobby eyes on head (fig. 4).

Games

The Queen of Hearts's House of Cards

The expression "house of cards" refers to a structure or situation that is on the verge of collapse. Just breathe a little too hard . . . and the walls come tumbling down! For this activity, all you need are six decks of cards. It's best to set the game up on a smooth, flat floor. (This avoids an opponent's temptation to shake the table.) Divide decks in half and give each child a stack of cards. The contest is to see who can construct the largest (and longest-lasting) house. Intentional sneezing, coughing, or stomping can disqualify an architect from the competition. If foul play is suspected, the following penalty may be called out: "Off with her head!"

Mad Hatter's Hat Rack

For this game, you'll need a hat or coat rack with enough hooks for several hats. Hang any variety of styles on the rack: from bonnets to berets, baseball caps to cowboy hats, straw hats to stocking caps, a formal top hat to a classic fedora. The more styles to choose from, the more fun.

Place the hat rack at one end of a large room (or backyard). Divide children into two teams and line them up side by side at the opposite ends of the room.

One by one, players from each team race to the hat rack and pick out a hat. They put on the hat, run back to the team, and put it on the head of the next player. Every new player must wear their hat to the hat rack and exchange it for a *different* hat before running back. (If a hat falls off en route, a player must go back to the hat rack and replace it with yet another hat.) The first team to finish wins the relay.

Pin the Grin on the Cheshire Cat

The elusive Cheshire Cat's omnipresent smile never seemed to fade. Long after he disappeared, his grin kept glowing. This game is based on the classic principles of pin the tail on the donkey: only the tail is a toothy smile (fig. 1) and the donkey is a cardboard cat (fig. 2). This works with the same blindfold principle as the classic game. Be sure to cut enough cardboard smiles for each player and write their names on the back. The one who gets the mouth in the right place (or closest to it) wins.

The bigger you make the cat, the more places there will be to misplace the mouth. You can make the entire cat, or just an extremely large cat face. Either way, 2' x 3' is a good size to work with. Find a large piece of corrugated cardboard, or cut one from the side of a large box. Draw a simple cat figure or face on the

Fig. 1

Fig. 3

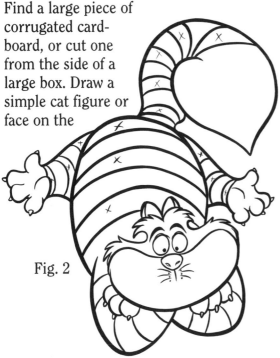

Fig. 2

board, and cut it out. Paint board light gray, with dark gray stripes (like a tabby). Paint on eyes and nose, but no mouth (fig. 1 or fig. 2) and hang the cat up on a tree trunk (or on an indestructible wall in the house). Then cut big "cheesy" smiles from a piece of poster board, outlining teeth with a Magic Marker (fig. 3). Push a white thumbtack in the center of the teeth. Children take turns being blindfolded and trying to pin the grin in the right place. (Sometimes it even ends up in an upside-down frown.)

Note: Adult supervision is necessary. Keep a careful count of the thumbtacks!

Beauty and the Beast Party

—— Age 4 to 8 ——

An enchantress turns a rude prince into a beast and his servants into animated household objects. For the spell to be broken, the Beast must learn to love another person and win that person's love in return. In a nearby village lives Belle, a strong-willed young girl with a passion for books and a desire for adventure. One day, her beloved father becomes the unwitting captive of the Beast in his castle, and Belle bravely offers her own freedom in exchange for that of her father. An unlikely love begins to unfold between Belle and the Beast. Their relationship, once based on captivity, gives way to one of mutual respect, caring, and, finally, love.

One of the things that really makes this party fun is treating the kids like guests at your "chateau." You, and any other parents helping out, can wear aprons and white caps. Dad can dress like a butler. Pull out their chairs, tuck in their napkins, and wait on them hand and foot! You can even give the birthday girl a little bell to ring for service. (Believe me, this is the best part of the party. When I was seven, my friend invited me to a "fancy lunch" at her house. When I arrived, we dined on a lace tablecloth, with the good china and silver. The menu was last night's roast beef. We kept her mom running in and out of the kitchen by ringing our little service bell. It was a blast!)

Beauty and the Beast Party

Invitation

Cogsworth the Clock

Decorations

Country French Motif

Lace tablecloth, books with potted geranium bookends, candelabra, individual roses
under clear plastic cups, scattered rose petals, animated plates and flatware

Get-Acquainted Activity

The Magic Mirror

Fantasy Feature

French Feather Dusters

Games

Once Upon A Time . . .
Dust Bunny Derby
Pass Mrs. Potts

Menu

Invitation

Cogsworth the Clock

With the hands on his face, Cogsworth the clock tells children what time to "be our guest."

Materials:

12 (8") brown paper party plates
24 (8½" x 11") sheets white paper
black felt-tip marker
stapler
12 (9" x 12") white envelopes
Yield: 12 invitations

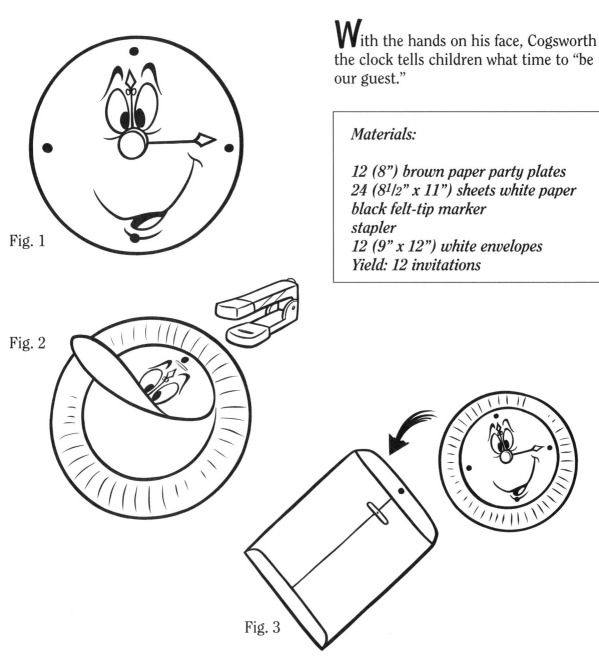

Fig. 1

Fig. 2

Fig. 3

Directions:

1. Cut out twenty-four 6-inch circles from the white paper.
2. On twelve of the white circles, draw Cogsworth's face, making the hands point to the time of the party (fig. 1).
3. On the other twelve circles, write the following message:

> *Cogsworth says*
> *it's time to*
> *"Be our guest!"*
> *Join Belle and* (your child's name)
> *for a*

Country French Feast
at
the Beast's Castle
(address, time, and date)
RSVP: (your phone number)

4. Place a circle with Cogsworth's face over a circle with the party message, and place both circles over the center of a plate.
5. Staple them together at the top (fig. 2).
6. Repeat this with each plate, and mail the invitations in oversize envelopes (fig. 3).

Preparation time: 1¹/₄ hours

Decorations

Country French Motif

Belle's favorite room in the castle is the library, so cover the table with a paper lace tablecloth, and use bookends to stand several books up in the middle of the table. Clay pots filled with red geraniums add to the French-country flavor and make great bookends, too. By all means, include a candelabra if you have one.

Don't forget the famous fading rose underneath the bell jar. You can have one for each place setting. Just tuck a real (or artificial) rose bud under upside-down clear plastic cups. For added effect, why not scatter loose rose petals around on the table. If you want edible roses, try cutting red fruit roll-up candy into 1¹/₂-inch-wide strips. Roll up strips and spread apart like a blossoming rose. Finally, "animate" the plates and flatware. If you're using plastic knives, forks, and spoons, cut 1-inch circles from white or colored paper. Use double-stick tape to attach the circles to the fronts and backs of the flatware handles and make faces on them with felt-tip markers.

Get-Acquainted Activity

The Magic Mirror

Cloistered in his lonely castle, the Beast's only window on the outside world is a magic mirror.

This is an activity where kids can join in as they arrive. It's really a simplified version of charades. Fill a glass bowl or jar with "rose petals" cut from red construction paper. On each petal, write names of characters or objects from *Beauty and the Beast*, things found in castles or even France. (Always keep the age-group in mind when coming up with ideas.)

Gather the kids around a full-length "magic" mirror. Each player takes her turn pulling a rose petal from the glass bowl. She then must draw a clue on the mirror (with a watercolor marker) about the character or object on her rose petal. She cannot actually draw the character or object. As soon as someone guesses what it is, it's their turn to pull a rose petal from the bowl and draw a clue on the mirror. Be sure to have spray glass cleaner and a rag handy to wipe the mirror between turns.

Fantasy Feature

French Feather Dusters

The French feather duster makes a fun party favor. In addition, children get to use them in the Dust Bunny Derby game. An assembly line setup is the best way to create these feather dusters, doing each step for each duster in turn before moving on to the next step.

Beauty and the Beast Party

Materials:

12 wooden paint-mixing sticks
    (from hardware or paint store)
4-inch colored feathers (about 2
    dozen for each skirt)
3/4" or 1" wide colored plastic tape
12 sets of plastic doll eyes with
    movable pupils (from craft or
    hobby shop)
2 feet 1/2" lace
12 colored tassels with 2" cord loops
acrylic paints
glue
scissors
Yield: 12 feather dusters

Fig. 1

Fig. 2

Fig. 3

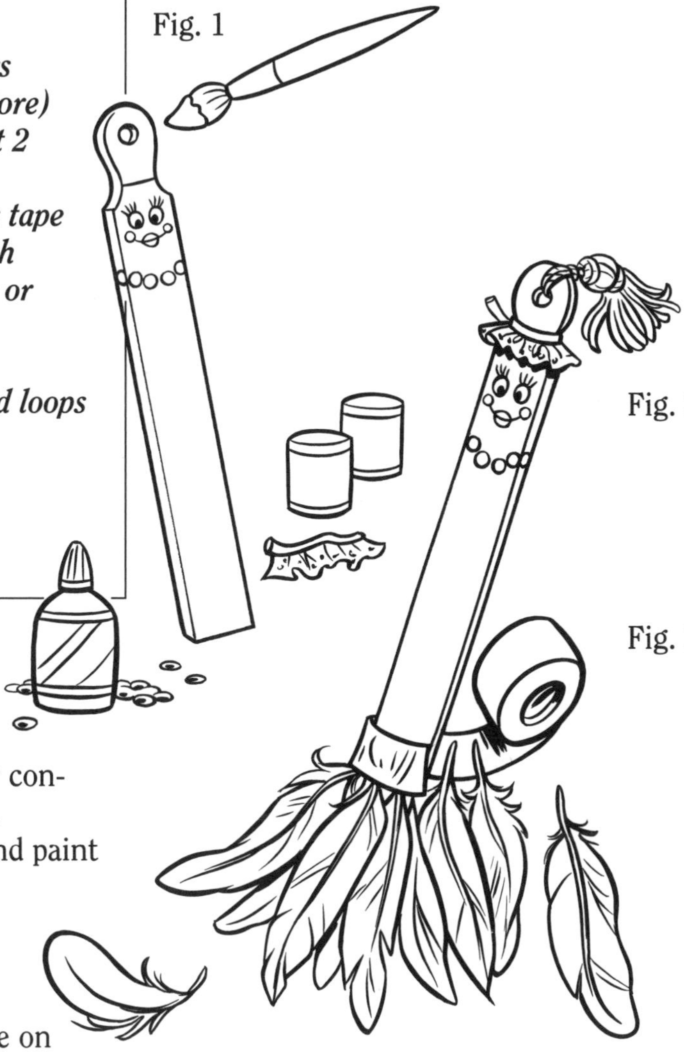

Directions:

1. First paint a hat on top of
   each stick handle (in the
   desired color, to coordinate or contrast with the feathered skirt).
2. Glue the eyes below the hat and paint
   red lips and a necklace to
   match the hat (fig. 1). Allow
   the paint to dry.
3. Flip the stick over and
    continue the hat and necklace on
   the back. Again, allow the paint to dry.
4. Glue a strip of lace around the front
   and back of each hat brim.
5. Loop a tassel through the hole in the
   hat (fig. 2, top). (If there are no holes
   in your sticks, drill them before
   painting.)
6. Begin taping feathers around the stick,
   starting two inches from the base of
   the stick. Tape six feathers around the

stick for the first layer (fig. 2, bottom).
7. Tape six more feathers around the handle for the second layer. Continue
   winding the tape around the stick several more times.

Preparation time: 1 3/4 hours
Drying time for paint: 8 hours

Games

Once Upon A Time . . .

Belle loves to read, and she marvels at the Beast's vast library. Here's a chance for party guests to write their own books for Belle!

In this group writing exercise, the result is laughter, not literary greatness. Each author is issued a cardboard report cover filled with twelve blank pages (the number of pages should correspond to the number of children at the party). Each author makes up a title and begins on the first page with "Once upon a time," followed by the beginnings of a story. When the first page is full, each author passes the book to the author sitting next to him or her. That person continues the story on the next page. Pages three through twelve progress the same way. When the books have gone full circle, they will return to the original authors, who pen "The End" and sign their names. Afterward, the authors take turns reading their books aloud. Children love to giggle at the crazy composite creations, especially when they recognize their own passages.

Note: These books make adorable party favors if you use fabric glue to cover them with felt. Glue a red satin ribbon rose (available at fabric shops) on each cover. Use a tube of fabric paint to write: "ONCE UPON A TIME . . . by (child's name)."

Dust Bunny Derby

This is a race that works well on a long paved driveway. If you are playing indoors, add several laps to the race to make it more exciting. Use cotton balls for dust bunnies. Divide the children into four groups. (This makes it easier to keep track of which dust bunnies belong to which child.) Children in each group line up at the starting line. At the signal, the first four children sweep their dust bunnies, with their French Feather Dusters, in a race to the finish line. Then the next two groups of four take their turns. The winner from each participates in a championship race.

Pass Mrs. Potts

This game works a lot like musical chairs, without chairs and without the children actually walking around. Instead, children sit in a circle with their backs to each other. All you need is a toy (or unbreakable) teapot and the musical score from *Beauty and the Beast*. As soon as you start playing "Be Our Guest," the kids start passing around the teapot. When the music stops, the child holding the teapot leaves the circle. (The child who has to leave does get to control the music for the next man out, and so on.) Of course, the circle gets smaller and smaller until it's down to just two players pitted against each other in a teapot passing play-off!

Aladdin Party

___ Age 5 to 9 ___

Leave it to Disney to reinvent a classic tale and give it a whole new life of its own. Such is the case with the smash hit *Aladdin*. From the amusing singing Genie to the evil Jafar, the film delights children and adults alike.

Just like the movie, this party is full of fun surprises. Kids come to explore the Cave of Wonders, ride on magic carpets, and dine at a sultan's feast. And they can hypnotize each other and ask a genie to grant their three fondest wishes. Even the food has a Middle Eastern flair in a kid-friendly way. Take for example PRINCE ALI KABABWA KABOBS WITH SULTAN'S SAUCE (page 137). These are really skewered hot dogs with pineapple, green peppers, and a "special sauce," served with pita bread and JASMINE'S CURRIED COUSCOUS (page 138).

Aladdin Party

Invitation

Genie in a Lamp

Decorations

Arabian Motif

Magic carpet tablecloth, sultan's palace centerpiece, balloon genies,
camel plates and cups, Rajah's Crispy Rice Tigers, Popcorn Cobras

Get-Acquainted Activity

Cave of Wonders

Fantasy Feature

Rajah's Crispy Rice Tigers or
Popcorn Cobras

Games

Magic Carpet Race
Hypnotized
Three Wishes

Menu

Prince Ali Kababwa Kabobs with Sultan's Sauce......137
Jasmine's Curried Couscous......138
Aladdin's Agrabah Market Ambrosia......139
Rajah's Crispy Rice Tigers......140
Popcorn Cobras......141
Genie Guice......139
Magic Carpet Cake......184
Abu Ice Cream......196

Invitation

Genie in a Lamp

Just like a genie crammed into a magic lamp, this invitation greatly expands upon opening.

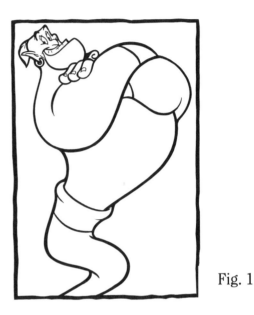

Fig. 1

Materials:

12 sheets of (20" x 30") blue tissue paper
black felt-tipped marker
12 (3" x 5") unruled index cards
12 (3" x 5") envelopes (or size to accommodate cards) any color
gold-ink writing pen
gold glitter glue writing tube
Yield: 12 invitations

Directions:

1. Make genies out of tissue paper by drawing a top-heavy body and a trailing tail with marker, using the entire sheet of tissue (fig. 1). Trim close to lines.
2. Use gold-ink pen to write the following message on cards:

Fig. 2

YOUR WISH IS MY COMMAND!
Come to Agrabah and . . .
Explore the Cave of Wonders
Ride a Magic Carpet
Dine at a Sultan's Feast
at the Palace of (your child's name)
at (your address)
on (date) *at* (time)
RSVP (your phone number)
Come Dressed in Arabian Duds

3. Fold up a tissue paper genie around each card and slip into an envelope.
4. Use gold pen to address envelopes on the front, then turn to the back and write "OPEN SESAME" across the top.
5. Seal envelopes. Use glitter glue, as you would sealing wax, only "draw" a small Aladdin-type lamp with the glue (fig. 2).

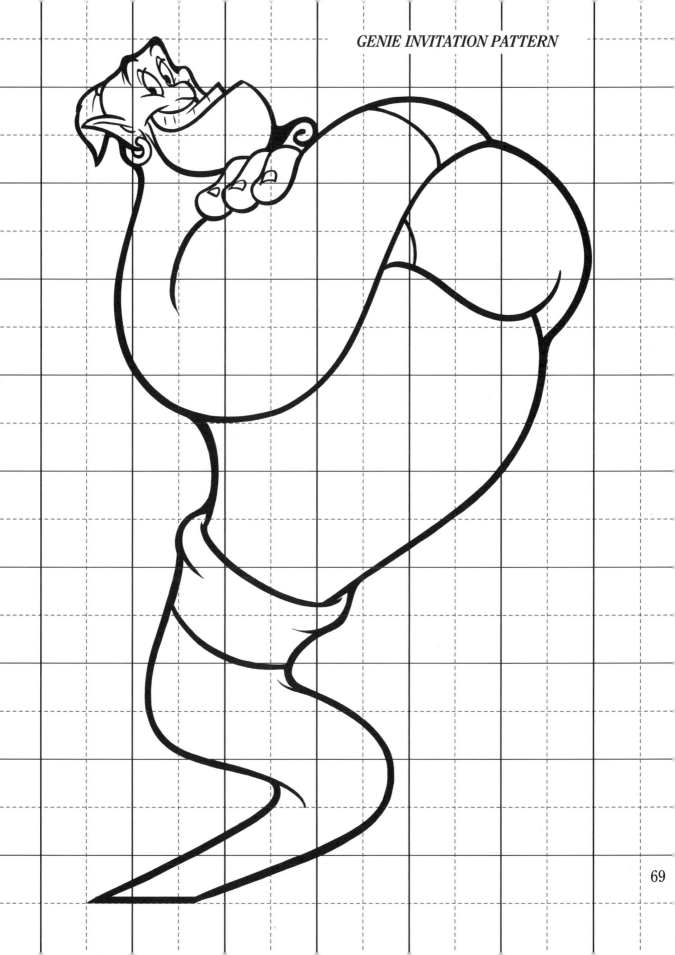

Decorations

Arabian Motif

Set the mood right at the table. Use paint or felt-tip markers to decorate a plastic or fabric tablecloth to look like a magic carpet. Add tassels to the corners so that it resembles an oriental carpet.

You can make a centerpiece that looks like a sultan's palace. All you need are some paper towel tubes, a shoe box, tear-drop–shaped Christmas ornaments (for towers), glue, and paint. The shoe box is the main building. Glue tubes on the top and sides. Paint and allow to dry, then glue on Christmas ornament towers. If you're good at twisting balloon animals, try your hand at making blue balloon genies. Use crayons to decorate plates and cups with camels. Decorate place settings with RAJAH'S CRISPY RICE TIGERS (page 140) and POPCORN COBRAS (page 141).

Get-Acquainted Activity

Cave of Wonders

As soon as guests arrive, usher them into the Cave of Wonders, which is any room in your house that lends itself to an eerie decor. Start by draping opaque plastic drop cloths (or sheets) over furniture. Dim the lights, draw the shades, and illuminate the room with strings of colored lights. Sprinkle sequins around to give the illusion of jewels everywhere. Paint or draw a tiger-god face on cardboard and tape it on the door to the room.

Inside the cave you'll scatter around treasures for each child to hunt down. The important thing is that all children get the same collection of favors and that each is tagged with their name. For example: You give a bag of gold foil-covered chocolate coins, a bracelet made of hard candies, and some sort of shiny trinket.

Each guest is admitted to the cave as soon as they say the secret password, "OPEN SESAME." After they've searched through the cave for their personally labeled treasures, they can carry them out (as long as the name on the tags matches theirs).

70

Fantasy Feature

Rajah's Crispy Rice Tigers or Popcorn Cobras

Recipes for these food favors are in a special section in the back of the book: RAJAH'S CRISPY RICE TIGERS (page 140) and POPCORN COBRAS (page 141). You can make one or both. Or, use these as a project in place of the get-acquainted activity or a game.

Games

Magic Carpet Race

You'll need to play this game on a smooth floor, such as linoleum or hardwood, so that the "magic carpets" can slide along the surface. To simulate magic carpets, use either two oriental-style throw rugs or heavy-duty bath towels with tassels sewn on the corners. Divide the children into two teams. Both teams line up, parallel to each other, at one end of the room. The magic carpet is given to the front of each line. The first player in line drags the carpet, while the second player in line rides on it. At the starting signal, the magic carpets race each other to the opposite side of the room. The carpet rider must tag the wall, jump off the carpet and switch places

with the carpet dragger. On the return trip back to the team, the former dragger gets to ride the carpet. As soon as they reach the team, the next two players take the carpet and the players who had their turn retire to the end of the line. The action continues until the first team finishes, with all players having had a turn. Kids really go wild for this kind of game, so you might want to play several rounds.

Hypnotized

Jafar used his golden cobra staff to hypnotize the Sultan (or anyone else he wanted to control). You can make a cobra staff by covering a cane with gold florist foil. Glue on movable hobby eyes and sequins for jewels. The game works a little like Simon Says. One child starts off as Jafar and takes possession of the cobra staff. The other players line up side by side across from Jafar. (The difference between this game and Simon Says is that only one child is ordered to carry out an action at a time, as opposed to all of them at once. Jafar points his staff at a player and gives commands such as "Jafar says hop up and down." The player must then hop up and down until Jafar says "Jafar says to stop." However, if Jafar simply said "Hop up and down" or "Stop," and the player still follows the command, that player is out and must sit down. The last player left standing gets to be the next Jafar.

Three Wishes

Ah, the "magic triad." Whether you catch a leprechaun or find a genie in a lamp . . . you always get three wishes. And there are rules, as the Genie explained to Aladdin: "I can't kill anybody, I can't make anybody fall in love with anybody else, and I can't bring people back from the dead." And of course, you can't wish for more wishes!

For this game, you'll need a magic lamp. Consider using a gravy boat or something similar. (For example, I have a tarnished teapot from an old silver service that looks like a genie is ready to jump out!) Remind them of the three rules and give each child three small strips of paper on which they write three separate wishes, fold them up, and stuff them inside the magic lamp. One child starts off as the Genie and the rest sit in a circle around him. The Genie draws a slip of paper from the lamp and reads a wish aloud. The Genie gets three guesses as to whose wish it is. As soon as the Genie identifies the rightful owner of the wish, the Genie is free and trades places with that player. If the Genie draws a wish that was written by himself then he must remain silent and slip it back into the lamp for another turn. By the way, there's another rule to this wishing game: All players must fess up to their wishes! Of course, long, drawn-out periods of giggles and silence are part of the fun.

Toy Story Party

___ Age 5 to 9 ___

Just as Disney pioneered the first feature-length animated film, they brought computer animation to the cutting edge. *Toy Story* is a triumphant marriage of artistry and technology. This breakthrough motion picture keeps both kids and their parents coming back for more. Children see their world of fast food and video arcades along with their parents' world of Slinky and Mr. Potato Head.

This is a party about a birthday party. What could be more appropriate! It's an R. C. (remote control) car rally, it's a claw machine, it's a wacky lunch from Pizza Planet, it's a mutant toy factory, but most of all, it's a piece of everyone's childhood.

Invitation

Virtual Realty Sign

Decorations

Andy's House

For sale sign, toy soldiers in hallway and on table, baby monitor, blocks,
toys, cowboy tablecloth, cloud plates, cups, and napkins

Pizza Planet

Christmas lights, stars and planets on ceiling and tablecloth, cardboard rockets,
fast-food containers, pinball and video games, menu board

Get-Acquainted Activity

Mutant Toy Factory

Fantasy Feature

Pizza Planet Popcorn Aliens

Games

Hot Potato Head
R. C. Car Rally
Claw Machine

Menu

Toy Story Party

Invitation

Virtual Realty Sign

Moving is one of the more difficult transitions in a child's life. The fact that moving day coincided with Andy's birthday made it a bittersweet celebration. However, it was the premise to *Toy Story*'s plot. So a real estate sign actually makes a perfect imaginative invitation.

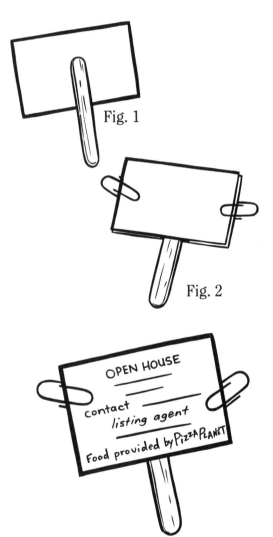

Fig. 1

Fig. 2

Fig. 3

Materials:

24 (3" x 5") unruled index cards
12 popsicle or craft sticks
colored felt-tip markers
black felt-tip marker
glue
paper clips
12 (6" x 9") envelopes
Yield: 12 invitations

Directions:

1. On half of the cards make a real estate sign using different colored markers for the lettering. The front of the sign should read:

> *FOR SALE*
> *VIRTUAL REALTY*
> *listing agent*
> (your child's name)

2. Glue the stick to the back of card (fig. 1). Use black pen to write the invitation on

the other half of the cards:

> OPEN HOUSE
> (your address)
> (date) (time)
> *contact* (your child's name)
> *listing agent*
> (your phone number)
> **Food provided by PIZZA PLANET**

3. Glue invitation to stick and edges of sign front, lining up evenly.
4. Secure edges in place with paper clips while drying (fig. 2).
5. Remove clips (fig. 3) and mail in envelopes that have been decorated with a Virtual Realty logo.

Decorations

Andy's House or Pizza Planet

Toy Story is a natural for children's party decorations. Most of what you need is already around the house! Start by making a full-size FOR SALE sign that matches your invitation. Stake it out in the front yard and tie balloons to the sign the way realtors do for an open house. (You never know . . . you might even get an offer! If you don't find inquiries amusing, wait about ten minutes until party time to post the sign.)

You can line up armies of toy soldiers around the stairs or in the hallway to spy on incoming guests. Kids can even announce their arrival on a baby monitor or walkie-talkie that's received by the kids over at the MUTANT TOY FAC-TORY table.

The party table itself can be decorated like Andy's Room or Pizza Planet, which-ever you or your child prefers. For Andy's Room: use blocks, toys, plastic sol-diers, dinosaurs, Slinkys, and a Mr. Potato Head. The table-cloth can actually be a cowboy bedsheet. Paint white clouds on sky blue plates, cups, and napkins. For Pizza Planet, you'll want to create the illusion of a space arcade. Dim the lamps and illuminate the room with strings of small white or colored lights. Tape up foil stars and planets on the ceiling. Cover the table with a dark blue plastic or paper tablecloth and make stars with silver glit-ter. Build rocket ships by covering oat-meal cartons or cardboard tubes with construction paper. Glue on nose cones and tail fins. Serve food in carry-out boxes, similar to a fast-food restaurant. Pinball and video games add to the atmosphere. Post the Pizza Planet spe-cials on a menu board.

Get-Acquainted Activity

Mutant Toy Factory

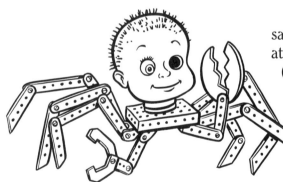

sadism as much as an expression of cre-ativity. Of all the mutant toys, Baby Head (with its creepy crew cut) reminded me of my doll, Sue Ellen, after my bro-ther styled her hair.

For this activity, you'll want to collect lots of broken toys, pieces from board games, Legos, Erector Set parts, screws, nuts, bolts, rubber bands, and lots of play clay so that kids can stick things together. Be sure to sup-ply plenty of doll parts, which are sold at craft stores for doll making.

I wasn't at all surprised to learn that the mutant toys were a huge hit with kids. Watching Sid on the screen brought back memories of my own dear brother dis-mantling all his toys (and mine) for Frankenstein-like experiments! Let me reassure parents that it's not a sign of

Set everything up on a special table. As the guests arrive, usher them into the MUTANT TOY FACTORY.

Fantasy Feature

Pizza Planet Popcorn Aliens

When Buzz Lightyear wound up at Pizza Planet, he got in with a crowd of strange characters—the three-eyed aliens inhabiting the claw machine. What you'll make here are just like those except they're made out of popcorn balls. For the recipe, check out PIZZA PLANET POPCORN ALIENS (page 144) in the Fun Food chapter.

Games

Hot Potato Head

Poor Mr. Potato Head was always having his face fall off. This potato would suffer similar mishaps, except that his face is painted on. (You wouldn't want to toss plastic parts through the air!)

Find a large baking potato and use acrylic paint to make a face on it. For this game, you'll also need a cowboy hat.

One child starts off as Woody, and wears the cowboy hat. The rest of the players gather in a circle around Woody. Woody closes his eyes and tosses the potato out to one of the players in the circle. (Woody's eyes must always remain closed.) The kids toss the potato randomly, from player to player as quickly as they can get rid of it. (As if it really were a red-hot baked potato.) At any point, Woody can call out, "Hot potato head!" The player left holding the hot potato is out. The circle grows smaller and smaller. The last player left becomes the next Woody in another round.

R. C. Car Rally

Ever since their invention, kids of all ages love R. C. cars. (As an adult, I find them addictively fun and my dogs think they're thrilling!) This game tests the players "driving skills." To add to the challenge, the cars have to carry some kind of passengers on top, just like Woody and Buzz Lightyear in *Toy Story*. If you don't have two R. C. cars, borrow one or ask one of the party guests to bring theirs. Select two dolls or figures of some sort that can easily ride on top of the cars with a sense of balance. (In all fairness to both teams, the dolls and cars should be about the same size.)

Divide children equally into two teams. Each team sits on opposite ends of the room, side by side. Make two "traffic cones" out of orange poster board. Put them in the middle of the room, about ten feet apart. Each team works left to right, meaning that the player on the left end of the line starts off with the remote control. The object is for the kids to drive the cars around the cones in a figure eight. If at any point a player knocks over a cone or the passenger falls off of the car, that player must reset the traffic cone or retrieve the passenger and place it back on the car, then turn the remote over to the next player on his team. The action continues like this down the line. Obviously there will be lots of crashes, many of them intentional! Everybody should get a chance to drive. However, the team that finishes first will obviously show the greatest skill.

Claw Machine

Who hasn't felt as frustrated as Sid when foiled by a claw machine? You can simulate this Pizza Palace arcade experience for a party game. For the machine itself, fill a large glass aquarium with trinkets and candy bars. Throw in "dud" prizes as well, things like tooth brushes or individually wrapped bars of soap that kids wouldn't want. Kids line up in front of the claw machine, and the first player in line is blindfolded and given a pair of kitchen tongs. Whatever they pull up is what they get. As soon as a player takes a turn, they go to the back of the line and the next player up is blindfolded and given the tongs. The game goes on and on until the claw machine is empty. *Note:* Kids can't pull up several prizes at once. If they do, they can only keep one prize, and if it's a dud prize . . . that's what they have to keep! The other prizes have to be dropped back into the box.

Pocahontas Party

Age 6 to 10

Disney's interpretation of *Pocahontas* is a tribute to a strong, free-spirited young woman. The film also celebrated the power of nature and a wealth from the land that was greater than gold. *Pocahontas* is also a romance that grade-school girls really relate to. In many ways, she's a contemporary role model from another time. It's no wonder that *Pocahontas* costumes are so popular. Who wouldn't want to be a beautiful, independent princess who can dive off a cliff into a river with the grace of a swan? Everything about *Pocahontas* is magical, including her love for the handsome Englishman, John Smith.

Invitation

Compass Card

Decorations

Native American Motif

Native American dolls, necklaces, and moccasins; arrangements of Indian corn, gourds, squash, logs, and foliage; trail of round crackers to your door; Indian-style blanket tablecloth; beadwork designs on plates, cups, and napkins; arrowhead place-markers

Get-Acquainted Activity

Indian Jewelry Workshop

Fantasy Feature

Brown-Bag Buckskin Vests

Games

Chicahominy River Canoe Race
Digging for Gold
Spinning Arrow

Menu

Pocahontas Wild Turkey Pyes......145
Indian Corn......146
Powhatan's Totem Pole Potatoes......127
Grandmother Willow Tree Tea......147
Percy's Peanut Butter Pug Cake......175
Meeko's Ice-Cream Raccoons......197

Invitation

Compass Card

Pocahontas was haunted by a recurring dream, a dream about a spinning arrow. It turned out to be symbolic of John Smith's compass, pointing her down another path.

Materials:

24 (8") paper plates (all the same color)
12 (6") paper plates (white)
9" x 12" sheet of black construction paper
12 brass brad fasteners
black felt-tip markers (wide- and fine-tip) scissors
glue or rubber cement
hole punch
6 yards of gold gift-wrapping cord
12 (9" x 12") envelopes
Yield: 12 invitations

Directions:

1. Glue a white paper plate in the center of half of the colored paper plates (fig. 1).
2. Cut arrows from construction paper that are about 4 inches long and a half-inch wide.
3. Poke a hole in the center of each arrow with a brad and then fasten it through the center of a plate (fig. 2).
4. Use wide marker to write letters of directions: N, E, S, and W.
5. Write the following message on the second half of plates with fine-tip marker:

The Spinning Arrow Points to a Pocahontas Party
Follow the Path to
<u>(your child's name</u>*)'s Village*
in the Virginia Forest
<u>(date, time, your address)</u>
RSVP: <u>(your phone number)</u>

6. Position compass plates on top of invitation plates.
7. Punch a hole at the top above the N, through both plates.
8. Cut gold cord into 18-inch lengths and tie each in a loop with a knot at one end (fig. 3).
9. Loop cords through hole, resembling the chain on a compass or pocket watch (fig. 4).
10. Address envelopes before sealing invitations inside, since the compasses are somewhat lumpy.

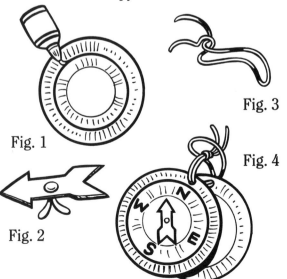

Fig. 1

Fig. 2

Fig. 3

Fig. 4

Decorations

Native American Motif

When decorating for a Pocahontas party, look to Native American culture as an inspiration. Any dolls, necklaces, or moccasins will add to the atmosphere. If you're celebrating indoors, invite nature inside with seasonal arrangements (Indian corn, squash, gourds, pumpkins, pinecones, cattails, birch logs, branches, and foliage). You can even bring out artificial evergreen that you might have been storing from the holidays. However you achieve the look, you want to feel like you're in a Virginia forest.

Let guests follow a trail of round crackers from the drive to your door (just like John Smith's hard tack biscuits).

The party table itself can be on the floor: Spread out an Indian-style blanket or decorate a plastic or paper tablecloth to look like one. Use grass mats and natural-colored paper plates, cups, and napkins (decorate with crayons or markers to resemble Indian beadwork). For place markers paint children's names on cardboard arrowheads and tie them to twigs like arrows.

Get-Acquainted Activity

Indian Jewelry Workshop

Pocahontas's favorite accessory was a striking necklace that had once belonged to her mother. When I first saw the film, I just knew every little girl would have to have one. With this Indian jewelry workshop, the party guests can copy the original or design their own.

There are several options for going about this. One would be to use craft beads and suede laces, which are readily available at craft shops. Another option is to use cord and dry pasta shells that have been colored with felt-tip markers to resemble beads. The third option is to make the necklaces edible. Use licorice laces and LifeSavers or Froot Loops cereal. Whatever you decide, set everything up at a special station, separating the beads by colors. If using pasta, give kids markers to color their own beads. If you use candy or cereal, have plenty to spare. Much of it will end up in their mouths instead of around their necks.

Fantasy Feature

Brown-Bag Buckskin Vests

You could spend a small fortune making vests out of synthetic suede or you could use this brown bag approach. I find that children are fascinated when simple things are transformed into something special. Remember to get very generic-looking bags without printing on them. Check with your local supermarket or buy a couple dozen from a paper supply outlet. Reinforcing openings and seams with masking tape makes the bags much stronger. Put out crayons or markers at the workshop and let kids decorate them as part of the get-acquainted activity.

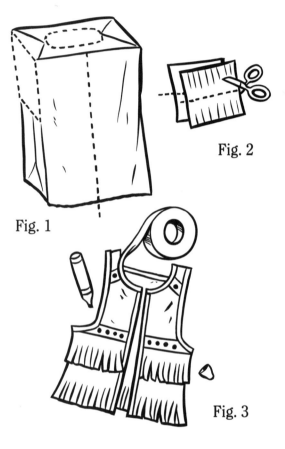

Fig. 1

Fig. 2

Fig. 3

Materials:

*12 (11$^{1}/_{2}$" x 7" x 13") brown paper
   bags (plain)*
$^{3}/_{4}$" masking tape
scissors
pencil
crayons
Yield: 12 vests

Directions:
1. Turn grocery bags upside down.
2. Split bags open in front, down the center, and cut about an 8-inch oval neck hole across the top (fig. 1).
3. Cut out arm holes from side panels of bags, about 7 inches down, giving you

two 7" x 7" scraps of paper (fig. 2). Reserve these for front fringe.
4. Reinforce diagonal shoulder seams (front and back) with masking tape. Ease tape around arm holes, folding in half over edge like a seam binding.
5. Do the same down the front and around the neck hole (fig. 3, top).
6. Cut 2-inch-deep fringe around the bottom, about a half inch apart.
7. Split reserved squares into 3$^{1}/_{2}$" x 7" strips.

8. Cut 2-inch fringe at half-inch intervals, and tape panels on front and back, lining panels up with arm holes.
9. Use crayons to draw beaded designs on the vest and on taped seams. Edge binding seams can use a sort of faux blanket stitch (fig. 3, bottom).

Preparation time: 15 minutes per vest

Games

Chicahominy River Canoe Race

Powhatan once told Pocahontas that "rivers are steady—steady as the beating drum." But Pocahontas disagreed. She told her father, "Rivers aren't steady at all. They're always changing."

Powhatan respected her wisdom and skill. He knew she could guide her canoe with ease, through the roughest waters.

Kids love this relay race because they get to travel down the Chicahominy River rapids on "sea-worthy" skateboards.

All you need for the game are two skateboards. The "river" can be any smooth area like a driveway or recreation room floor. Use fireplace logs or other objects to create an obstacle course or "rapids."

Divide children into two teams. Line up each team at one end of the river. The first player on each team sits, cross-legged, on a skateboard. The object is to push the board along using your hands as paddles. At the starting signal, players canoe downstream (around the logs) and return upstream along the same course. When a player reaches the shore, the next in line takes over the canoe and paddle.

The first team to finish the relay wins.

Digging for Gold

Governor Ratcliffe felt certain that the New World was filled with gold, and he became frustrated when none could be found. John Smith searched for words to explain the precious metal to Pocahontas saying, "It's yellow and comes out of the ground. It's very valuable." Then Pocahontas reached into her bag and pulled out an ear of corn. "Here," she said handing it to him, "we have lots of gold."

Part of the wisdom here is that money has no meaning if there's nothing to eat, and that the riches of nature are the greatest wealth of all. As John Smith said, "One look at this beautiful place and the men will forget all about digging for gold."

You can play this game outside or indoors with a plastic wading pool filled with popcorn. You'll need six ears of uncooked corn, six chocolate coins, and large spoons for each child to use as a shovel. Bury the corn and coins at the bottom of the pool. At the signal, let the digging begin.

Rule #1: Players cannot dig with their hands.
Rule #2: Players cannot shovel the popcorn out over the side of the pool.
Rule #3: Players may not stand in the pool.

As soon as a player finds a chocolate coin, they win a bag of chocolate coins (and then retire with their wealth). If a player finds an ear of corn, they win a prize. Everyone wins something because no one can keep two prizes. Perhaps the best prize of all is getting to wallow around in a pool of popcorn!

Spinning Arrow

Pocahontas confided in the wise old tree, Grandmother Willow. She was particularly puzzled by a recurring dream: "I dream that I am running through the woods. Then right there before me is an arrow. As I look at it, it begins to spin." According to Grandmother Willow's analysis of the dream: "Child, it seems to me this spinning arrow is pointing you down your path."

This game is really more of a recreational activity than a competition. Most grade-school girls could play this all afternoon because they love sharing the seemingly silly symbols in their dreams and trying to unlock the mysteries they reveal. All you need is a "spinning arrow." The arrow can be made from a dowel with the arrowhead end indicated with red paint. This needs to be played on a smooth, flat surface, so test the dowel to be sure it will spin. One player starts off as Grandmother Willow. She spins the arrow until it stops on a player in the circle. Grandmother Willow then assumes a treelike stance. The player picked by the arrow consults Grandmother Willow about the meaning of a dream. As soon as the tree gives her analysis, she takes a place back in the circle and the player selected by the arrow becomes the next Grandmother Willow.

The game goes on and on like this. Players always have the option to pass on a turn if they can't think of a dream to talk about . . . but this never seems to happen!

Sleeping Beauty's Disney Princess Pizza Party

Slumber parties are a rite of passage for grade-school and preteen girls. A special bonding takes place that seems to be part of growing up. Food is an important part of these parties because the girls tend to eat like famished wolves. They also enjoy making their own refreshments as an entertainment activity.

This is what I call a mix-and-match party. Although much of this chapter is based on the *Sleeping Beauty* theme of Princess Aurora, Prince Philip, and the evil fairy Maleficent, you can use elements from many Disney parties. For example, heroines from other chapters influence the menu. Feel free to borrow games and activities from any part of the book as well. Or, let the girls come up with their own inspirations!

Sleeping Beauty's Disney Princess
Pizza Party

Invitation

Castle Card

Decorations

Medieval Motif

Brown wrapping paper tapestries and flags, cardboard shields, foil swords, foil-covered throne

Get-Acquainted Activity

Peanut Butter Popcorn Palace

Fantasy Feature

Magic Wands

Games

Scary Fairy Taleathon
Spinning Yarns
Resting Royals

Menu

Belle's Baguette's (French Bread Pizza)......135
Jasmine's Pineapple Pita Pizza......147
Pocahontas Pizza......148
Peanut Butter Popcorn Palace......149
Glass Slipper Soda......133
or Enchanted Hot Chocolate......148
Classic Disney Castle Cake......188
and/or Disney Ice-Cream Dream Castle......207

Invitation

Castle Card

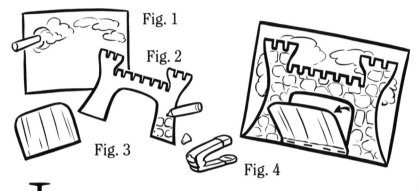

Fig. 1

Fig. 2

Fig. 3

Fig. 4

This all-purpose medieval castle invitation could be to the house of just about every Disney princess (with the exception of Pocahontas and Jasmine). But, of course, they have their very own parties, as well as namesake pizzas in this party.

Materials:

*12 sheets light blue construction
    paper*
*12 sheets beige or gray construction
    paper*
tracing paper
pencil
white chalk
scissors
black felt marker (fine tip)
brown felt marker (wide-chisel tip)
paste or rubber cement
stapler
12 (9" x 12") envelopes
Yield: 12 invitations

Directions:
1. On each sheet of the blue paper, smudge some chalk clouds around the top of the page (fig. 1). (These invitations are designed horizontally.)
2. With tracing paper and pencil, trace the castle card pattern on next page. Use this as a pattern to cut out twelve castles from the beige paper.
3. Cut out a section for the drawbridge (which will be reattached on the invitation), and draw stone walls onto the castles (fig. 2).
4. Draw wide boards on the drawbridge pieces using the brown marker (fig. 3).
5. Paste the castle onto the blue paper, and write the following message in each drawbridge opening:

Come to (your child's name)**'s Castle
and Stay Overnight for
Sleeping Beauty's Disney Princess
Pizza Party
at** (your address)
on (date and time)

6. Staple the drawbridge over the message at the base of the castle (fig. 4). The drawbridge flap should pull down.
7. Mail invitations in large envelopes.
Preparation time: 1 hour

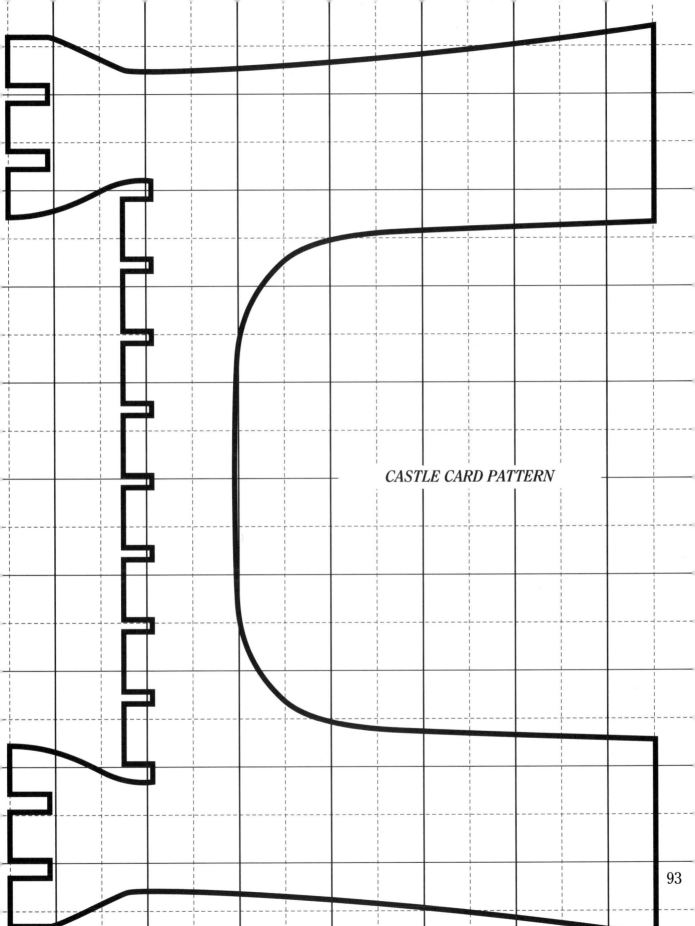

CASTLE CARD PATTERN

93

Decorations

Medieval Motif

For a Sleeping Beauty slumber party, think medieval. Look for any decorations that might add this feeling to your home. Begin by drawing tapestries on brown wrapping paper. These renditions can be murallike scenes from the story. (If you're not much of an artist, don't worry.) Hang tapestries on the wall, along with colorful cardboard shields and foil swords. A foil-covered chair makes a great throne. Medieval flags, also made from brown wrapping paper, are very dramatic when hung from the ceiling over the table. Paper plates and cups can be decorated with coats of arms (any design with castles, crowns, or lions). Finally, save room in the center of the table for the Peanut Butter Popcorn Palace that the girls will make.

Get-Acquainted Activity

Peanut Butter Popcorn Palace

Popcorn and slumber parties just seem to go together. Guests at this party gather in the kitchen to mold gooey globs of popcorn into a massive edible edifice that's fun to eat!

As the girls arrive, divide them up so that eventually there are three groups mixing up the recipe for PEANUT BUTTER POPCORN PALACE (page 149). Everyone joins together to build the actual palace and create the towers.

Fantasy Feature

Magic Wands

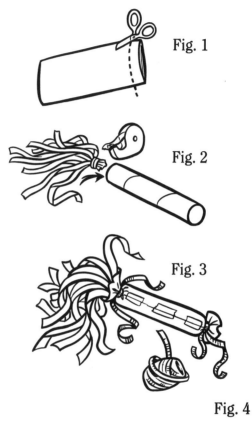

Fig. 1

Fig. 2

Fig. 3

Fig. 4

When the three good fairies Fauna, Flora, and Merryweather, waved their magic wands, they sent sparks flying everywhere and caused quite a commotion. A magic wand makes a marvelous slumber party favor—for casting spells on sleeping friends or for waking them up with bouts of harmless head-bonking! (Actually, it would be hard to hurt even a fly with a swat from one of these.)

Materials:

1 package rainbow cellophane sheets
1 package red cellophane sheets
1 package green cellophane sheets
1 package blue cellophane sheets
1 package gold cellophane sheets
12 empty paper towel tubes
scissors
tape
curling ribbon (any metallic color that coordinates with one of the tissues)
Yield: 12 wands

Directions:

1. For the streamers, remove all cellophane from the packages (except for the gold), and keeping the cellophane sheets folded, cut through all thicknesses, at 3/4-inch intervals (fig. 1).
2. Unfold the strips into streamers and divide the colors evenly into twelve bunches.
3. For each wand, gather the streamers at one end and tape them down inside the opening at an end of an empty paper towel tube (fig. 2).
4. Cut twelve 6" x 20" strips of gold cellophane and wrap them tightly around the cardboard tubes.
5. Tape closed along the seams (fig. 3). Tie off the ends with the curling ribbon (fig. 4).

Preparation time: 1 hour

Games

Scary Fairy Taleathon

Spooky stories and ghostly tales don't just happen on Halloween night—they're also part of the slumber party tradition. In this game, girls take turns weaving their own sagas of wicked witches, evil fairies, ferocious dragons, and dreadful dungeons. Everyone sits in a circle, the lights are dimmed, and a progressive story is begun. The sequence must start with "Once upon a time . . ." and be followed by a two- or three-sentence contribution from each storyteller. As the story goes around the circle, there's only one rule to the game. Somehow it all has to end up "happily ever after!"

PREVIOUS PAGE:

A POOH-STYLE PICNIC
Peanut Butter Pooh Cake, Baby Roo Jelly-
Bean Bags, and Owl Invitation

LEFT:

A PARTY ON THE SERENGETI
Personalized Pride Rocks and African
Acacia Invitation

SEEING SPOTS
LEFT: Dalmatian Invitation, Perdita's Chipper Ice Cream Pups, Hot Dogs in Bread-Bone Buns, and Dalmatian Dog Ears
Fantasy Feature • ABOVE: Dalmatian Invitation and Dalmatian Dog Ears Fantasy Feature

The invitation reads:

ARIEL INVITES YOU
UNDER THE SEA
TO A PARTY AMONG THE MERPEOPLE
FOR
SARA'S BIRTHDAY

OCT. 2ND. AT 1 P.M.
7 HANSON RD.

R.S.V.P. 379-

WELCOME TO NEVER LAND
OPPOSITE: Map to Never Land Invitation, Crocodile Coin
Clips Fantasy Feature, and Crocodile Cake

FUN UNDER THE SEA
ABOVE: Scallop Shell Invitation, Sebastian's Crab Cakes, and
Shells from King Triton's Shell Shop • **RIGHT:** Sebastian's
Crab Cake

The text on the invitation reads:

Princess Tina's
presence is requested
at the grand ballroom
of Rebecca's palace
for a royal birthday party
14 Brushy Hill
on May 27th at 1 p.m.
R.S.V.P. on royal phone line
322·8657

THE ROYAL BALL
ABOVE: See-Through Slipper Invitation and Golden Tiara Fantasy Feature
RIGHT: Classic Disney Castle Cake

A VERY HAPPY UNBIRTHDAY
OPPOSITE: Mad Hatter's Top Hat Invitation and
Marshmallow Magic Mushrooms

TALE AS OLD AS TIME
ABOVE: Disney Ice-Cream Dream Castle
RIGHT: Cogsworth the Clock Invitation and French Feather Duster
Fantasy Feature

A WHOLE NEW WORLD
OPPOSITE: Popcorn Cobra Fantasy Feature, Jasmine's Curried Couscous, and Prince Ali Ababwa Kabobs
with Sultan's Sauce.

YOU'VE GOT A FRIEND IN ME
ABOVE: Aliens and Virtual Realty Invitation

FIT FOR A PRINCESS

LEFT: Peanut Butter Popcorn Palace • ABOVE: Castle Card Invitation and Magic Wand Fantasy Feature

A HERCULEAN EXTRAVAGANZA
Ancient Greek Scroll Invitation, Herculade and Zeus Juice Boxes, and Laurel-Leaf Garland Fantasy Feature

Spinning Yarns

Spinning wheels seem to pop up all the time in fairy tales, from Rumpelstiltskin to Sleeping Beauty.

In this game, the girls pretend to be princesses in a spinning race. The players are divided into six teams to see who can unravel and then rewind a skein of yarn the fastest. Each pair sits opposite each other about six feet apart. One player unwinds a skein of fairly fine gauge yarn in a continuous line to the other player, who quickly works to wrap the yarn around her hands. If the yarn snarls or snaps, it has to be straightened or tied back together before the players continue. The first team to finish is crowned queen.

Resting Royals

When Princess Aurora pricked her finger on the spinning wheel and fell into a deep sleep, the good fairies decided to cast the same spell over the rest of the kingdom. Aurora and the royal court slumbered away, frozen in time. It was up to Prince Philip to awaken Aurora and bring the kingdom back to life.

This is essentially a shell game, using sleeping bags. One girl pretends to be Maleficent (the evil fairy) and leaves the room. The rest of the girls scramble about to hide deep inside someone else's sleeping bag. (For this scenario we're assuming that Maleficent would have wanted to foil the efforts of the good fairies and interrupt the sleeping court.) When Maleficent returns to the room, everyone pretends to snore. Maleficent walks from sleeping bag to sleeping bag, trying to guess who's underneath. She stops at each one and commands, for example, "Princess Hillary...wake up or die!" If it really is Hillary, she must wake up and come out of hiding. If it isn't Hillary, whoever it is "dies" (stops snoring). The last princess to die becomes Maleficent in the next round, when everyone switches sleeping bags again.

Hunchback of Notre Dame Party

Age 7 and Up

Welcome to the world of Quasimodo, where only he and the gargoyles share a bird's-eye (or should we say pigeon's-eye) view of the world. Oh, what a wondrous place it is, right below the bell tower lies the city of Paris! With the reverse revelry of Topsy-Turvy Day the Festival of Fools is the perfect party theme. October birthday? Halloween party? Look no further than the Court of Miracles for a spooky setting.

When it comes to party ideas, *The Hunchback of Notre Dame* has something for everyone. It appeals to a broad range of ages, especially the upper-level grade-school children who often think they've outgrown theme parties. Wait till they grow up and find out "big kids" still have silly parties. In fact, I might just use this theme for my next adult Halloween party!

Invitation

Esmeralda's Palm of Fortune

Decorations

Notre Dame Cathedral

Stained glass windows, bells, gargoyle statues

Topsy-Turvy Day

Paper banners, puppet theater, tents, tambourine plates, balloons, Floppy Felt Crowns

Court of Miracles

Graveyard setting with tombstones, skeletons, plastic rats and owl

Get-Acquainted Activity

King of Fools

Fantasy Feature

Floppy Felt Crowns

Games

Frollo's Frozen Gargoyles
Topsy-Turvy Races

Menu

Hunchback Honey-Glazed "Pigeon Wings"......150
Phoebus Phries with Bell Tower Tomato Sauce......151
Esmeralda's Ruby and Emerald Grapes
with Cheese Balls and Baguettes......152
Quasimodo Quencher......152
King of Fools Crown Cake......185
Do-It-Yourself Ice-Cream Gargoyles......199

Invitation

Esmeralda's Palm of Fortune

Fortune-telling was just one of the beautiful Esmeralda's talents. She could read a person's life by looking at the lines on his or her palm. By using your own hand as an outline, the pattern of a perfect invitation is right at your fingertips!

Materials:

12 sheets of peach-colored construc-
*   tion paper*
sienna-colored pencil or marking pen
fine gauge lavender tulle, cut into 12
(2" x 15") strips
scissors
stapler
12 (5" x 7") envelopes
Yield: 12 Invitations

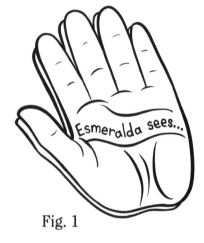

Fig. 1

Directions:
For this invitation, it's easier to write on an adult-size hand, so use your own palm as a pattern.

1. Trace around your hand once and cut out the outline. Simply use this as a template for tracing the rest. (Don't draw around your own hand each time, or you'll never get the fingers to line up the same way twice!)

2. You'll need to cut two matching pieces for an invitation from each sheet of paper.

3. Once you've cut out all of the hands, be sure all the thumbs are pointing in the same direction (left) while you write on them.

4. Study the creases across your own palm and fingers. Draw the major lines on one half of the paper palms (for top sheet) with the sienna pencil. Along the heart line write:

   Esmeralda Sees . . . (fig. 1)

5. On the second half of each pair of hands, write the following message in

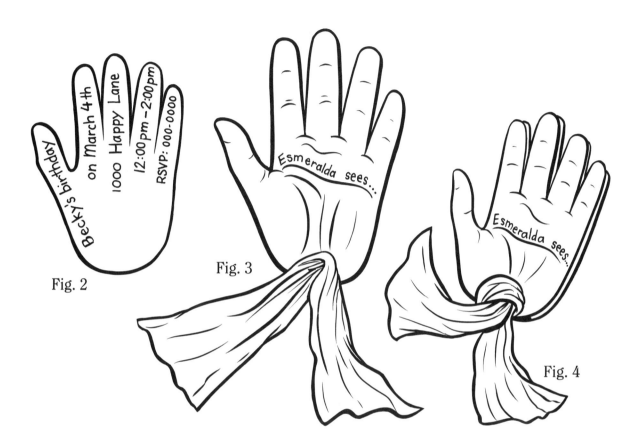

Fig. 2

Fig. 3

Fig. 4

the center of the palm. (Do not draw palm lines on second sheet.)

... A festival in your future. The city of Paris welcomes you, so come in your gypsy attire. "Good things come to those who wait . . . listen and follow."
Across the thumb write: (your child's name)*'s Birthday*
Across the index finger write: *on* (date)
Across the middle finger write: (address)
Across ring finger write: (time)
Across little finger write: *RSVP:* (phone number)

Refer to fig. 2.

6. Staple top and bottom sheets together at the base of palm, tacking a strip of tulle in the process (fig. 3).
7. Loop tulle in a loose knot to cover staple (fig. 4).
8. Address envelopes.
9. Fold scarf around hand so it fits into envelope.

Decorations

Notre Dame Cathedral, Topsy-Turvy Day, Court of Miracles

There are really three themes from *The Hunchback of Notre Dame* that can be incorporated into party decor. Use one or a combination. The most obvious is the cathedral itself. Create stained glass windows by cutting panels of colored cellophane and taping to your windowpanes. Tape various shapes or designs onto the solid panels. Hang large bells from the ceiling. (*Note:* If you can't find any cowbells or schoolhouse-type bells at a hardware store, there are always marine bells. An inexpensive alternative would be to make bells out of cans with wire spoons inside as clappers.) Look around at your local garden center for some gargoyle-like statues to guard your entrance. Or you can craft small gargoyles out of stone-colored clay and use them on the party table.

Then, of course, there's Topsy-Turvy Day in the town square. Colorful paper banners add the same atmosphere as this Parisian festival. A puppet theater or a striped bedsheet pitched like a gypsy tent gives a carnival illusion. Why not eat off tambourines? You can make them by punching holes around the rim of sturdy paper plates. Thread cord through the holes in the plates and string small cardboard circles to make bangles. When setting the table, don't forget to arrange all of the utensils backward and upside down. Tie balloons to the floor instead of the ceiling (kids love stepping on them). The Fantasy Feature, FLOPPY FELT CROWNS, double as place markers. Be sure to write each child's name *backward* on the hat!

Finally, if this party happens around Halloween, take advantage of the Court of Miracles motif. The setting is in the catacombs of a graveyard tomb. In October, it should be easy to find cardboard or crepe-paper skeletons to hang on the walls. With paper or fabric, you can put slipcovers on the backs of chairs to resemble tombstones. Write names and dates with markers. Plastic toy mice (for rats) or a decoy owl (used to scare off pigeons) really set the mood. Don't forget to dim the lights!

Get-Acquainted Activity

King of Fools

It's party time in Paris! You'll want to get each and every gypsy in the spirit as soon as they arrive. At the Festival of Fools, he who wears the ugliest mask is crowned king. Have a table ready where incoming guests can create their own masks. Consider using 5" x 8" brown paper bags. They're inexpensive and have limitless potential. Provide crayons, markers, construction paper, paste, and blunt scissors. Trim about 5 to 6 inches across the open end of each bag, shortening them to fit a child's head and neck. Tell the kids that their goal is to make the ugliest face; then you just sit back and enjoy the action! Have an unbiased party select three kids with the ugliest masks, then bring them up to a review stand for a final public vote. The wearer of the mask with the most "boos" from the crowd is crowned King of Fools. Make FLOPPY FELT CROWNS (below) from golden felt and jingle bells. For the review stand, refer to TOPSY-TURVY RACES (page 107).

A drum majorette baton can easily be transformed into a scepter. Cover it with gold florist foil, then add bands of ribbon for color accents. And don't forget the royal cape! This could be a purple bath towel fastened across the shoulders with a broach. (Of course, all of the kids at the party will want their very own floppy crown. That's why it's a fantasy feature. There's one with each child's name on it marking their place at the party table.)

Fantasy Feature

Floppy Felt Crowns

The King of Fools crown has that buffoonish look of a court jester's cap. You'll want to make one for each child and personalize it with their names (write backward, of course, in honor of Topsy-Turvy Day). When it comes time to crown the King of Fools contest winner, have a special crown ready that says: SLOOF FO GNIK!

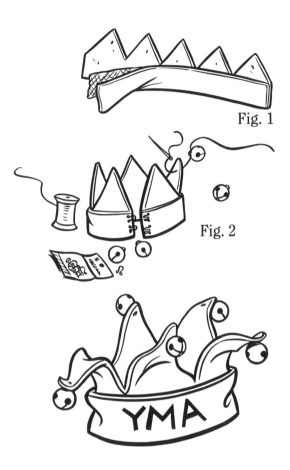

Fig. 1

Fig. 2

YMA

Materials:

5/8 yards 60"-wide golden yellow felt
5/8 yards 60"-wide red felt
1/4 yards 60"-wide purple felt
1 3/4 yards 45"-wide fusible fabric web
5 small jingle bells per hat (65 bells if making 13 hats, etc.)
glitter paint in writing tube
hook-and-eye fasteners
scissors
iron
needle and thread
Yield: 12 hats

Directions:

1. Enlarge crown pattern to scale. Since these are 20 inches wide and 5 inches high, you can cut a row of three from the 60-inch width of felt. (There's enough felt to make 16 crowns, if necessary.)
2. I find it's simpler to fuse the yellow and red felt, back-to-back, before cutting out the crowns. To do this, the length of your fusible webbing, 1 2/3 yards (or 60 inches) will line up with the width of your felt.
3. Trim the excess width of the webbing down so that it's even with the felt. (Reserve this piece for attaching bands.) The webbing should be positioned so that it's sandwiched between the red and yellow felt.
4. Follow manufacturer's directions for fusing felt together with your iron.
5. Use pattern to cut crowns out of yellow and red double-faced felt.
6. Cut 2" x 20" strips out of purple felt and 2" x 20" strips out of remaining fusible webbing.
7. Use iron and strips of webbing to fuse a purple felt strip along the lower edge (yellow side) of each crown (fig. 1).
8. Using your child's head as a guide, determine whether to join crown edge to edge or overlapping in the back. (This will vary according to age-groups.)
9. Sew on hook and eyes accordingly (fig. 2, bottom).
10. Sew bells on the tips of every point on each crown (fig. 2, top).
11. With glitter paint write the names of each child backward (see finished hat).

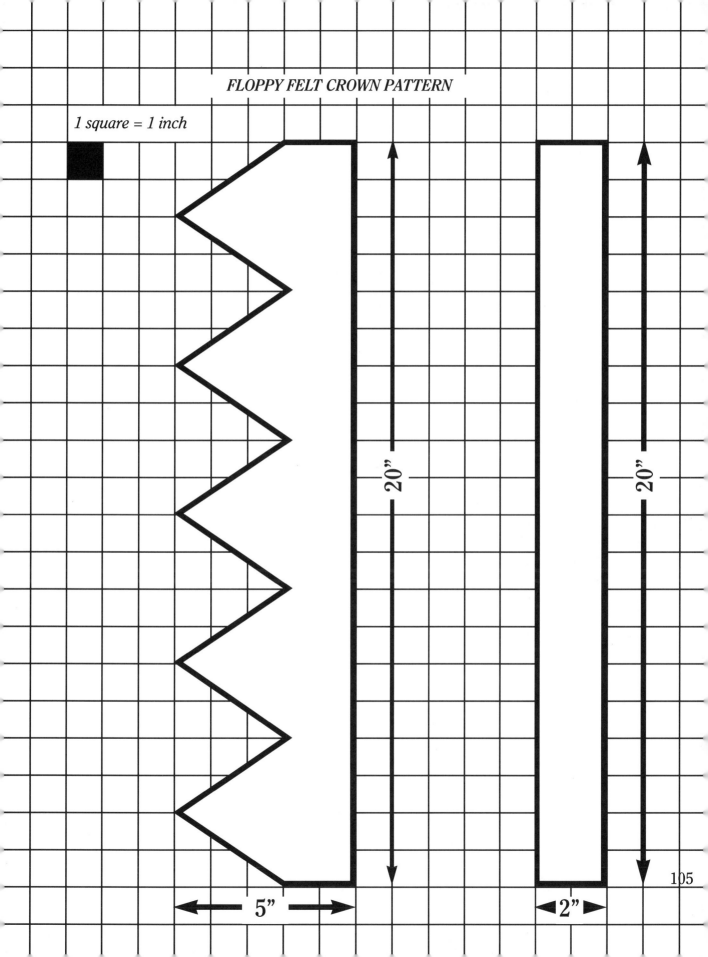

FLOPPY FELT CROWN PATTERN

1 square = 1 inch

20"

20"

5"

2"

105

Games

Frollo's Frozen Gargoyles

Work on Notre Dame cathedral took one and a half centuries to complete and the architectural masterpiece is covered with gracefully carved figures. It's been said that some are placed so high, "Only an angel can admire their details." But we know someone else! Gargoyles (best described as grotesque little statues resembling a hybrid goat-monkey-winged troll doll) came alive only in the presence of Quasimodo. When fiendish Frollo appeared, they returned to their inanimate state.

This game is really just good old-fashioned freeze tag with a twist: First, Hugo, Victor, and Laverne are legless statues. Children playing gargoyles must hop instead of run. Second, ice cubes are introduced to add to the excitement. Frollo is given a bag with as many ice cubes as there are circulating gargoyles. Quasimodo is given an empty plastic

bag. To even the score, both Frollo and Quasimodo must also hop. Frollo's objective is to tag as many gargoyles as possible. The frozen gargoyle must stand still, holding one of Frollo's ice cubes. If Quasimodo comes along, he can take away the ice cube (put it in his plastic bag) and unfreeze the gargoyle, bringing it back to life. While Frollo is distributing ice cubes, Quasimodo is collecting them. However, if Frollo should tag Quasimodo, Quasimodo must give back one ice cube. Of course, this is a race against the clock, since ice melts in hot little hands. Any gargoyle can also come back to life when their ice cube has completely melted. Eventually, all the ice will be gone. At that point, the game begins again with a new set of cubes. The last frozen gargoyle becomes the next Frollo, and Frollo becomes the next Quasimodo.

Topsy-Turvy Races

The Festival of Fools was also known as Topsy-Turvy Day because all things are reversed. In an absurd parade, a dog walks a man, a lobster cooks a chef in a pot, and a fish tries to reel in a fisherman.

This series of relay races is based on role reversal. Divide party guests into two teams. Paint "REVIEW STAND" on an orange crate and use it as a goal post. Teams line up side by side, with the review stand at the opposite end of the room or yard. For the first race you'll need two stuffed toy dogs and two leashes. Loop the handle of the leash around the leg of a stuffed dog. (A slipknot will give a secure grip.) The first kid in each line gets down on her hands and knees. The clip of the leash can be snapped on to either the child's shirt collar or belt. (The idea is for the stuffed dog to be "walking" the child.) At the signal "STOP," players at the front start crawling toward the review stand, dragging their dog "master" behind them. Teams always circle around the review stand from opposing approaches. (See diagram.) As soon as each player returns to their team, they go to the back of the line, unclip their leash, and pass it (along with the stuffed dog) to the front of the line. The first team to finish the relay is declared the winner and the next race begins. With the second relay, you'll need four "horse tails." For this purpose you can use a large tassel and clip it to the back of the player's pants (or skirt) with a clothespin. To form a headless two-tailed horse: the first two players in each line clip on their tassels and stand facing each other, holding hands. At the signal "STOP," each team's horse starts trotting toward and around the review stand. (Both ends of the horse get the opportunity to trot backward either coming or going.) When the horse returns to the rear of its team, players unclip their tassels and pass them down the line to the next two players. The first team to finish the relay wins. (*Note:* Because this race involves two kids at a time, you can run each team twice for more action.)

The third race is about reverse walking. Each team gets a pair of large mittens to wear on their feet. The first child in line takes off his shoes, puts the mittens on over his socks, and puts his own shoes on his hands. At the signal "STOP" the starting players walk backward around the review stand, taking care that their mittens don't come off their feet. (If one does, they have to go back for it.) When that player reaches the end of his team's line, he passes the pair of mittens up to the first kid in line. The first team to finish the relay wins.

Hercules Party

Ages 7 to 10

It's an A-list affair! Everyone who's anyone of mythological fame is invited to a birthday bash on Mount Olympus. Zeus and Hera host this party of all parties, presenting their son to the immortal's social scene.

This feast fit for the gods makes Hercules a great theme for your child's next birthday. It's a toga party (or should I say "pillowcase party") with all the trimmings.

Kids get to dine on fantasy Greek food and imagine what it would be like to live the life of an Olympian luminary. The menu offers an opulent selection for a celestial-style banquet. Of course, you may opt to serve just some of the dishes and also include your child's favorite foods.

Hercules Party

Invitation

Ancient Greek Scroll

Decorations

The Great Hall of Mount Olympus

Golden thrones, greek columns, lightning bolts, wooden bowls of grapes, cyclops plates

Get-Acquainted Activity

Pillowcase Tunics

Fantasy Feature

Laurel-Leaf Garlands

Games

Volcano Capping

Thread of Fate

River of Souls

Menu

Invitation

Ancient Greek Scrolls

The ancient Greeks wrote on scrolls of papyrus or parchment, bound at both ends to wooden rods. From proclamations to epic poems, just about everything was written in these roll-up books. What better way to send an authentic Olympian birthday announcement than on an authentic Greek scroll?

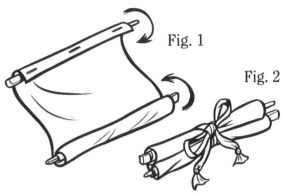

Fig. 1

Fig. 2

Materials:

1 sheet of graph paper
(bold) black felt-tip marker
12 sheets of parchment paper
12 pairs of chopsticks (no Chinese writing!) or 3/8-inch wooden dowel cut into 24 ten-inch lengths
medium-point felt-tip or calligraphy marker (available at art supply stores)
stapler
string or cord
scissors
12 8¹/2" by 11" envelopes or 12 mailing tubes
Yield: 12 scrolls

Directions:

1. Begin making invitations by blocking out a prototype on graph paper. The grids will help you center the message and line up the letters.
2. Use the bold marker to write the following message so that you can see the writing through the sheets of parchment:

> *The great Zeus and the goddess Hera Command your presence at a feast fit for the gods*
> *In celebration of* (your child's name)*'s birthday*
> (time and date)
> *At Mount Olympus*
> (your address)
> *RSVP:* (your phone number)
> *BYOP (Bring Your Own Pillowcase)*

3. Once you've made the master pattern, be sure the ink has completely dried before placing a sheet of parchment on top.
4. For each invitation, trace over the lettering using the marker or calligraphy pen.
5. Staple the narrow ends of the paper to the chopsticks or dowels (fig. 1).
6. Roll up and tie with a piece of string or cord (fig. 2) Address the envelopes before sealing the scrolls inside.

Decorations

The Great Hall of Mount Olympus

The perfect place for a Hercules party is at the Great Hall of Mount Olympus, where a feast fit for the gods is about to begin. Create golden thrones by wrapping chairs in gold florist foil or binding them with rolls of golden crepe paper streamers.

Surround the room with faux Greek columns, using brown wrapping paper sheets that are long enough to reach from floor to ceiling. Use white paint to create the columns. Once the paint dries, trim the paper around each column and tape them up along the walls.

Since Zeus (also known as the thunder god) was fond of throwing lightning bolts, why not "zap" some around the room? Simply cover zigzags of cardboard with aluminum foil. Hang these from the ceiling, suspended by fine thread.

Set up the feast down the center of the table and surround with wooden bowls of red and green grapes (compliments of Dionysus) and ATHENIAN AMBROSIA ALMOND CRUNCH (page 156). Decorate party plates by drawing a Cyclops eye in the center of each, using nontoxic crayons or markers. Cover juice boxes with HERCULADE or ZEUS JUICE labels.

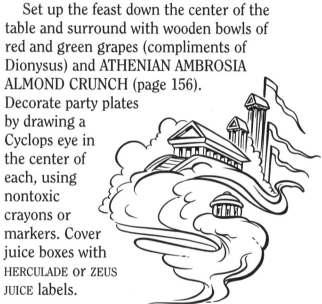

Get-Acquainted Activity

Pillowcase Tunics

When it comes to costumes, this is the original toga party! Rather than have the kids wrap themselves in yards of bedsheets, they'll have much more mobility in comfortable pillowcase tunics. The invitation indicates BYOP, so guests should arrive with a pillowcase. However, when the guests RSVP, you should suggest they bring a white one. Otherwise, some kids will arrive with stripes or flowers. Remind parents to provide kids with old pillowcases . . . unless they want to make the bed with a HUNK-ULES tunic!

Since Hercules spoofs modern merchandising, it's only logical that kids will want to sport HERC and HUNK-ULES logos on their togas. The best way to do this? Have guests make iron-on transfers using special crayons designed for this purpose. Kids won't have to worry about making a "mistake" on their tunic because they will draw their final design on paper with pencil.

In addition to the crayons, you'll need to provide paper and a smooth surface where the kids can work. Be sure to remind kids that words drawn on the paper will be reversed on the tunic! In other words, they'll have to spell (and letter) backward. You may have to help out younger children. Or, create a few logos yourself, photocopy them, and kids can just color them in.

When it comes to making the transfers, be sure to follow the manufacturer's directions for your crayons. Always brush away any stray crayon crumbs or there will be lots of unexpected spots when you make the transfers. Finally, make sure to set up your ironing board somewhere away from the party activity.

The tunics are created by cutting slashes for neck and arm holes (fig. 1). They're then tied at the waist with a cord (fig. 2). For extra fun, provide extra-long shoelaces so that kids can lace their sneakers up around their ankles like Greek sandals.

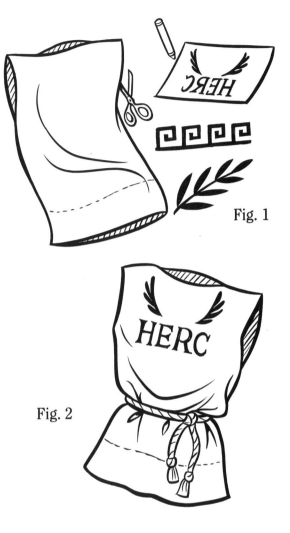

Fig. 1

Fig. 2

Fantasy Feature

Laurel-Leaf Garlands

Wreaths of laurel leaves were used to crown the heads of Greek gods, gifted scholars, and great heroes. These hats are easy to make and can be personalized with each guest's name. Or, you can assign the kids names of Greek mythological luminaries.

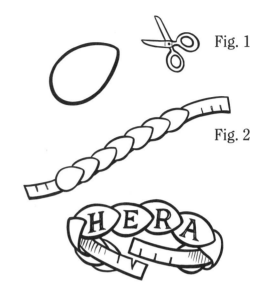

Fig. 1

Fig. 2

Materials:

20" x 30" sheet of green poster
    board
24 sheets of green construction paper
tape measure and ruler
pencil
scissors
glue
felt-tip marker or crayon
    (dark green or black)
Yield: 12 wreaths

Directions:

1. Measure your own child's head as a guide for that age-group. Add 3 inches to the measurement and cut twelve 1$\frac{1}{2}$ inch-wide strips of poster board that length.
2. Cut a leaf according to the pattern (fig. 1).
3. Use that leaf as a guide and cut as many leaves as you can from each sheet of construction paper.
4. Glue leaves across each headband (fig. 2), allowing 2 inches of uncovered poster board at each end.
5. Cut two slashes halfway through the band at both ends, but at one end cut from the top, and at the other end cut from the bottom (also see fig. 2) to form adjustable joints.
6. Write names across bands and join at the back by slipping notches together.
(See *Who's Who on Mount Olympus,* at right)

Who's Who on Mount Olympus
(The A-List)

GODS

Apollo	God of Light and Music
Ares	God of War
Hades	God of the Underworld
Hephaestus	God of Fire
Hermes	Messenger God
Poseidon	God of the Sea
Zeus	God of Thunder, Mightiest of the Olympians

GODDESSES

Aphrodite	Goddess of Beauty and Love
Artemis	Goddess of the Hunt
Athena	Goddess of Wisdom
Demeter	Goddess of Harvest
Hera	Goddess of Motherhood, Queen of the Olympians
Hestia	Goddess of the Hearth
Thetis	Goddess of the Sea

Games

Volcano Capping

One of Hercules' feats was plugging the top of an active volcano. Herc used a really big rock, but kids can do the same thing with a beach ball. All you have to do is make a volcano. This is much simpler than it sounds.

Find a wastepaper or trash basket with a round opening that's slightly smaller than the beach ball. The ball should rest on top of the wastepaper basket without falling inside.

Now that you have the basic structure, you need to make it look like a volcano. The easiest way to do this is to drape the basket with a large piece of fabric. (Boys' G. I. camouflage-pattern sheets give the volcano a great look, but if you don't happen to have any, another sheet will do, or check out the remnants section at your local fabric store.)

Center the fabric or sheet over the opening of the basket. Tuck the fabric down inside the basket, anchoring it in place with a brick or some other weight. (This helps pull the fabric down into the cavity and also keeps the volcano from tipping over.) Drape the fabric down around the sides so that it looks like a mountain with a hole on top.

The game begins with the children forming a line about five feet from the volcano. Each player takes a turn tossing the beach ball. If they "cap" the volcano (the ball rests on top), they go to the end of the line for another turn. If the player misses the volcano—or knocks it over!—they have to sit down. Once a round has been completed, the front of the line moves back a full step. This makes each turn progressively more challenging for the remaining players. The game continues until only one "hero" is left standing.

Thread of Fate

The three Fates controlled destiny. These haggard old crones shared one eye and could see the past, present, and future. They determined the length of a mortal's life by measuring a thread and cutting it at the moment of death. Even the mighty Zeus had no power over the Fates.

This game is sort of like hot potato. Instead of the players passing a potato around the circle, they pass the "thread of fate." One player, representing one of the Fates, controls the music. Since the Fates share one eye, this player's head is covered with a brown paper bag with a single large eye drawn on it. Don't cut an eyehole, though—the Fate isn't meant to see out of the bag. (If no one wants to be the Fate, put a grown-up in control of the music.)

The game begins with the other players sitting in a circle on the floor. The first player takes hold of the end of the thread and passes the spool to the left. The music plays as the spool makes its way around the circle. The minute the Fate stops the music, Mom or Dad cuts the thread at the spool, and the player holding the end of the thread "dies." That player drops out of the circle but keeps the thread. The game goes on until only one player is left. That player then becomes the Fate, and the player with the longest thread wins that round.

Note: Getting tangled thread is part of the fun, but for younger kids you can always use thick yarn.

River of Souls

The River of Souls (also known as Styx) was a murky river that flowed around the underworld. Sooner or later, all mortals had to cross the River of Souls to enter Hades' underworld. In charge of passage was the ferryman, Charon.

If the souls had money, Charon would take them across (that is why the next of kin would put a coin under the tongue of the deceased). Those who could not pay had to wander about in search of a pauper's entrance.

The "river" can be any defined stretch of space with a "bank" along each side. (A driveway works well for this, as does a quiet side street. If playing on the street, however, Mom or Dad will want to keep a lookout for cars.) A player is chosen to be Charon, the ferryman, who stands on one side of the river. Charon should have a small bucket (like a sand pail) for collecting coins. The players line up along the opposite riverbank. Each has been given a foil-wrapped chocolate coin (or a penny). They call out in unison, "Charon, take me across the River of Souls!" Charon calls back, "Not unless you have a golden coin for passage!"

Of course, no one really wants to give up their coin to pay for passage, so they all try to cross the river on their own. If Charon tags a player holding a coin, that player must put the coin in the fare bucket and then switch places with Charon. The players, including the original Charon, gather on the opposite riverbank and begin again.

In the following rounds, if Charon tags a "pauper" (a player without a coin), that player "drowns" in the river (sits out) and never reaches the underworld. Eventually, Charon will end up with all of the coins and everyone will have "drowned" except for one player who will win the bucket of chocolate change!

Note: When the original Charon joins the souls, he or she should have a coin for passage. Subsequent Charons, having had to pay a fare, will not.

Fun Food

Just because a party has a complete menu in this book, doesn't mean you have to serve the full meal. Many children are delighted with just cake and ice cream. Other kids insist on feeding their friends lunch.

Because a party is meant to be fun, it's not an appropriate time to play "food police." I'm all for feeding kids broccoli forests in a home setting. However, this strategy often falls flat in front of the peer group. So as not to embarrass your child or waste money on rejected food, stick with the familiar. That doesn't mean you can't give hamburgers, hot dogs, pizza, and pasta funny names and creative presentations. Believe me, they'll eat it up.

Nutrition and Preparation

Nutrition is of great concern to most parents these days. In addition to favorite finger-friendly foods, I've included a section on side dish coleslaws, potatoes, and fantasy fruits. These are almost always universally accepted by children. If you wish to cut fat from recipes, you can substitute low-fat alternatives. Reduced fat mayonnaise or yogurt can be used in many recipes, as well as low-sodium or reduced-fat cheeses. Even ground beef can be replaced with ground turkey. All of the recipes in this book are geared to serve twelve kids, but you can cut the recipes in half, or double them to suit your party.

A Note About Toothpicks

Toothpicks are often an essential part of party food construction. Always be sure to remind children of their presence in a food or to remove them before allowing kids to eat. Two great alternatives for anchoring soft foods together are pieces of dried spaghetti or small, thin pretzel sticks.

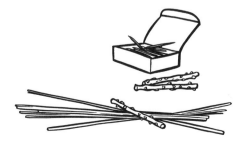

Pooh Bear's Biscuit Burgers with Honey Mustard

Winnie the Pooh Party

12 SERVINGS

Ingredients:

4 cans extra large refrigerated biscuits (8 count)
1 egg, beaten with 1 tablespoon water
4 dozen blanched almonds
6 dozen raisins
2 dozen 1-ounce hamburger patties
Honey Mustard (use store-bought or see recipe that follows)

Fig. 2

Fig. 1

Preheat oven to 400°F. Open the cans and separate the biscuits. Place twenty-four biscuits on ungreased baking sheets, about 2 inches apart. Cut each remaining biscuit into three equal-size pieces (fig. 1). Brush whole biscuits with egg, and roll biscuit pieces into balls. Press one ball into the center of each biscuit, and lightly brush with egg. Push two almonds, pointed ends out, into the top of each biscuit for ears. Use raisins for the eyes and nose (fig. 2). Bake for about 10 to 12 minutes, or until golden brown. Cool slightly and then split each biscuit in half. Grill or broil hamburger patties and serve on biscuits with pots of Honey Mustard on the table.

HONEY MUSTARD:

Ingredients:
1 cup brown mustard
1/2 cup honey
1/2 cup regular or reduced-fat mayonnaise
1 tablespoon lemon juice

Combine ingredients in small mixing bowl and blend until smooth.
Preparation time: 20 minutes
Baking time: 10 to 12 minutes

Orange-Pineapple Owls

Winnie the Pooh Party

12 SERVINGS

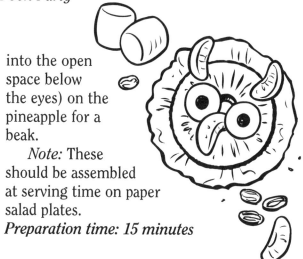

This very wise salad combines kids' favorite fruits into a friendly face. Arrange the pineapple rings on the lettuce leaves. Place two orange segments at the top of each pineapple ring to resemble the feather tufts of a great horned owl. Flatten marshmallows into ¼-inch patties. Place on the pineapple rings for eyes. Use raisins for pupils, pushing them into the marshmallows. Place an orange segment (so that it tucks into the open space below the eyes) on the pineapple for a beak.

Note: These should be assembled at serving time on paper salad plates.

Preparation time: 15 minutes

Hundred-Acre Wood Honey-Apple Punch

Winnie the Pooh Party

Combine 1 gallon apple cider with 1 quart lemonade and ½ cup honey in a punch bowl. Add a 2-liter bottle of club soda or sparkling water before serving.

Hot Dogs in Bread-Bone Buns

101 Dalmatians Puppy Party

12 SERVINGS

These frankfurters, wrapped in breadsticks to resemble dog bones, will delight the dalmatian pups at the party—even though they bake up big enough for a Saint Bernard!

> *Ingredients:*
>
> *12 franks*
> *3 cans (8 count) refrigerated bread-sticks*
> *1 egg*
> *1 tablespoon water*

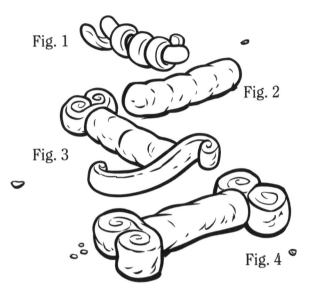

Fig. 1

Fig. 2

Fig. 3

Fig. 4

and split it in half. Press the center of each strip firmly into the end of each frankfurter. Then roll the ends of the dough toward each other to resemble the knobs of a bone (fig. 3). Place bones 3 inches apart on a baking sheet that has been sprayed with nonstick coating. Beat the egg with 1 tablespoon water and brush each bone with the mixture. Bake for 20 minutes or until they are puffy and brown (fig. 4). Serve them warm on plates with Pongo's Pears and condiments.

Note: These are best when wrapped and baked immediately before serving. The uncooked dough does not keep well in the refrigerator. If you must make these the night before, bake them, refrigerate, and then reheat them in a 250°F just until heated through.

Preparation time: 20 minutes
Baking time: 20 minutes

Preheat oven to 350°F. For each bone, unroll the breadsticks and wrap one around each frankfurter (fig. 1). Stretch the dough and pinch the seams together to completely conceal the frank (fig. 2). Unroll another breadstick for each frank

K-9 Krunchies

101 Dalmatians Puppy Party

12 SERVINGS

Pongo and Perdita's pups love to watch television. Their favorite show is *Thunder*, about a sheriff's dog in the wild, wild West, and their favorite commercial is for "K-9 Krunchies" dog food. They know the jingle by heart (and I'll bet your child does, too!).

Ingredients:

8 cups potato chips
4 cups corn chips
4 cups cheese puffs
K-9 Krunchies Box (the secret
ingredient: instructions follow)
Personalized Dog Dishes
(instructions follow)

Fig. 1

Fig. 2

Combine snacks in a large bowl and pour into K-9 Krunchies Box. (If there's some left over, just save it in the kitchen for refills.) To serve, pour from box into individual dishes.

K-9 KRUNCHIES BOX
Simply cover an empty economy-size cereal box with solid-colored wrapping paper. Use markers to create your own dog food logo on the box (fig. 1).

PERSONALIZED DOG DISHES
Buy small plastic pet food bowls at a pet shop. Use acrylic paint to personalize with each child's name (fig. 2). These make great place markers and party favors.

Pongo's Pears

101 Dalmatians Puppy Party

12 SERVINGS

Most small children love fruit salads. Canned pears and prunes make this one easy and economical.

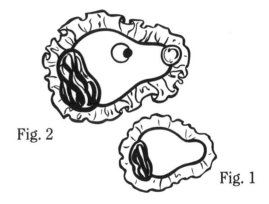

Fig. 2

Fig. 1

Ingredients:

12 lettuce leaves (green leaf or Boston)
12 premium-quality (large) canned pear halves
6 canned prunes
12 miniature marshmallows
12 raisins
6 Concord (purple) grapes

Place the lettuce leaves to one side of the lunch plates. (Hot Dogs in Bread-bone Buns will be served alongside this dish.) Drain the liquid from the pears and place them cut-side down on the lettuce leaves.

Split the prunes in half, lengthwise, and remove the pits. Place the prune halves at large ends of pear halves for ears (fig. 1). Cut small holes in each pear for an eye and push in marshmallows. Press raisins in the marshmallows for the pupils. Split the grapes in half, crosswise, removing the seeds. Set one grape half at the end of each pear for a nose (fig. 2).

Note: These take so little time, there's no need to prepare them in advance.
Preparation time: 15 minutes

Chocolate Chip Dog Biscuits

101 Dalmatians Puppy Party

12 SERVINGS

You can make these cookie dog bones ahead of time, or turn it into an activity (page 13). Just remember to use this dough. Commercial cookie dough contains eggs, and the bones will expand into unrecognizable blobs!

Preheat oven to 300°F. Cream shortening, butter and sugar in a large mixing bowl. Blend in flour. Mix in regular chocolate morsels (miniature chocolate morsels are for decorating). Divide dough into twelve equal balls.

Line a baking sheet with parchment paper. Roll each ball into a log shape. Flatten and shape into a dog biscuit. Place on parchment paper and decorate with miniature chocolate morsels to spell names or add extra spots. (*Note:* You can let children shape their own dough, or shape the dough yourself and let them decorate with chocolate morsels.)

Bake for 25 to 30 minutes, or until edges are firm but cookies are not browned. Cool completely before removing from baking sheet.

Preparation time: 15 minutes
Baking time: 25 to 30 minutes

Ingredients:

2/3 cup shortening
2/3 cup butter or margarine, softened
2/3 cup sugar
1/2 teaspoon almond extract
3 1/3 cups flour
1 (16-ounce) bag Nestlé Toll House Semi-Sweet Morsels
1 (12-ounce) bag Nestlé Toll House Mini Morsels

Polka-Dot Milk

101 Dalmatians Puppy Party

Divide a 6-ounce package of chocolate morsels between sections of four ice cube trays.

Fill trays with milk and freeze. Serve ice cubes in glasses of milk (allow 1 gallon and 1 quart).

Wildebeest Burgers with Serengeti Sauce

The Lion King Party

12 SERVINGS

Kids love these hamburger buns with horns!

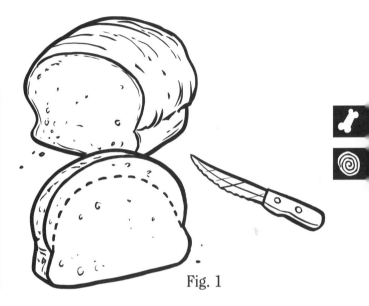

> *Ingredients:*
>
> *12 slices pumpernickel bread (about*
> * 5 1/2" x 3 1/2") from a 1 pound loaf*
> *12 3-ounce hamburger patties*
> *12 hamburger buns*
> *toothpicks, pieces of dried spaghetti,*
> * or small pretzel sticks*
> *Serengeti Sauce (recipe follows)*

Fig. 1

Before cooking hamburgers, make wildebeest horns from pumpernickel bread. Cut a narrow crescent from the curved part of each slice, tapering at ends (fig. 1). Grill or broil hamburgers until done. Put patties in buns. Anchor pumpernickel horns on top of buns using toothpicks, spaghetti, or pretzels (fig. 2). Serve with Serengeti Sauce.

SERENGETI SAUCE:

> *Ingredients:*
> *1/2 cup bottled barbecue sauce*
> *3/4 cup regular or reduced fat*
> * mayonnaise*
> *1/4 cup onion relish*

Fig. 2

Combine ingredients in a small bowl and blend until smooth.

Preparation time: 20 minutes

Pride Rock Potatoes

The Lion King Party

12 SERVINGS

Ordinary tater tots become a roaring new taste sensation with a sprinkling of sesame seeds and a hint of spice. Don't worry about picky eaters: there's no such thing as an exotic french fry! These are willingly wolfed down.

> **Ingredients:**
>
> *1 (32-ounce) bag frozen potato puffs*
> *1/4 cup sesame oil*
> *1 tablespoon curry powder*
> *1/2 teaspoon salt*
> *1/4 cup sesame seeds*

Preheat oven to 400°F. Put the frozen potatoes in a large mixing or salad bowl. In a separate bowl, stir the curry powder and salt into the oil. Pour the mixture over the potatoes and sprinkle in the sesame seeds. Gently toss until the potatoes are evenly coated. Spread them into two jelly-roll pans and bake for about 20 minutes (shaking to turn while baking) until golden and crisp. Transfer the potatoes to paper towels to drain off any excess oil. Serve them warm.

 Note: These can be baked in two batches if your oven is small. They can also be held in a warm oven for about an hour.
Preparation time: 5 minutes
Baking time: 20 minutes

Orange Elephants

The Lion King Party or Aladdin Party

12 ELEPHANTS

These make a fun parade of pachyderms around the party table.

> **Ingredients:**
>
> *12 navel oranges*
> *4 dozen large marshmallows*
> *toothpicks (see note, page 117)*
> *2 dozen miniature marshmallows*
> *2 dozen whole cloves*

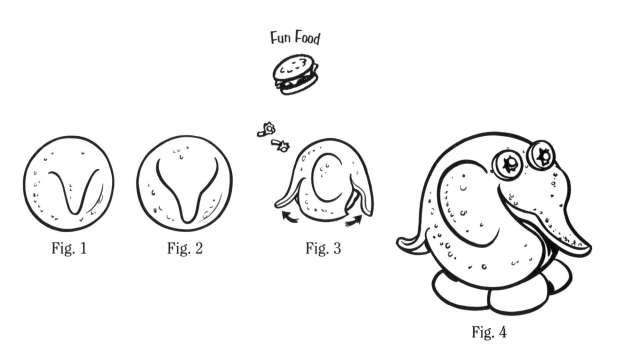

Fig. 1   Fig. 2   Fig. 3

Fig. 4

For each elephant, make a V-cut just above the orange's stem end for the tail (fig. 1). Carve a Y at the other end for the trunk (fig. 2). At each side, make C-shaped cuts for ears. Gently pull all cut peel slightly away from the orange (fig. 3). With toothpicks, attach four large marshmallows to the bottom of each orange for legs. Flatten the miniature marshmallows to form the eyes. Insert clove stems for pupils through the center of each marshmallow, and push them into place on the orange (fig. 4).

Note: These are best prepared the morning of the party.

Preparation time: 25 minutes

Pumbaa Punch

The Lion King Party

Combine 1 gallon of pineapple juice with 1/2 gallon limeade. Serve in cups with slices of kiwi on the edge.

125

Pirate Ship Poor Boys

Peter Pan Party

12 SERVINGS

With paper sails, carrot curl flags, and olive portholes, these poor boys make very convincing pirate ships. Good enough even for Captain Hook!

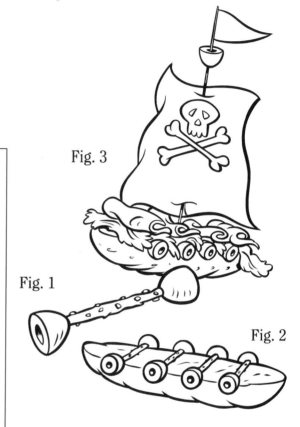

Fig. 3

Fig. 1

Fig. 2

Ingredients:

6 hero or grinder rolls (6" to 8" long)
1/3 cup mild mustard
4 1/2 dozen black olives
4 dozen thin pretzel sticks
12 lettuce leaves (green or red leaf)
2/3 cup regular or nonfat mayonnaise
2 pounds deli-sliced ham or turkey
   (extra thin)
12 (9") wooden skewers or strong,
   thin plastic straws
12 paper pirate sails (instructions follow)
12 carrot flags (instructions follow)
white paint

Split rolls in half, lengthwise, and spread with mustard. Make a slit in the closed end of each olive and insert one end of a pretzel stick into the slit. Each pretzel stick should have two olives on it (fig. 1). Line up four pretzel sticks with olives on each roll for portholes (fig. 2). Place lettuce leaves on top of each roll and spread with mayonnaise. Arrange the deli slices in a folded fashion on top of the lettuce. Insert skewers through the paper pirate sails to make billowing sails, and add an olive crow's nest near the top of each skewer. Stick a carrot flag on the tip and insert one skewer in the center of each sandwich (fig. 3).

To make carrot flags, cut thin slices, lengthwise, from peeled carrots. Cut one end to a point to resemble a flag. Soak in ice water for several hours (or overnight) until pieces become slightly wavy. To make pirate sails, cut twelve sails from black construction paper (6 1/2" x 3 1/3" at the base, tapering to 2 1/2" at the top). Paint skull and crossbones with white paint on sails.

Preparation time: 25 minutes

Tiger Lily's (or Powhatan's) Totem Pole Potatoes

Peter Pan Party or Pocahontas Party

12 SERVINGS

These roasted red-skinned potatoes are like eating baked potatoes on a stick. Fierce or funny faces are carved on each potato, then they're skewered together to look like totem poles. These are perfect for a Peter Pan Party or a Pocahontas Party.

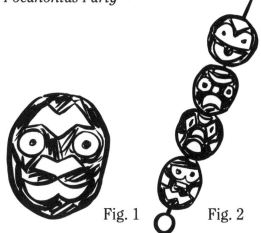

Fig. 1   Fig. 2

Ingredients:

4 to 5 dozen red-skinned potatoes
12 skewers
1 to 2 tablespoons olive oil
whipped butter or margarine and/or sour cream and chives

Wash and scrub potatoes. Using a small paring knife, carve faces into the potatoes. Try to vary expressions. Pieces of potato can be cut away to form eyes, nose, and ears (fig. 1).

Preheat oven to 375°F. Skewer four or five potatoes on each stick (fig. 2) and place in a jelly-roll pan. Brush with olive oil and bake about 45 to 50 minutes, turning two or three times. Serve hot with butter and/or sour cream on the side.

Preparation time: 20 minutes
Baking time: 45 to 50 minutes

Tinkerbell's Tangerine Punch

Peter Pan Party

Combine 1/2 gallon tangerine juice with 1/2 gallon of lemonade.

Under the Sea Biscuits

The Little Mermaid Party

12 SERVINGS

Tuna salad on biscuits shaped like scallop shells makes for thematic—and pretty!—bite-size sandwiches. (For those landlubbers at the party, fill a few biscuits with cheese spread.)

Ingredients:

2 cans (10 count) or 3 cans (8 count) extralarge refrigerated biscuits
1 egg, beaten with 1 tablespoon water
King Triton's Tuna Salad (recipe follows)
2 (5-ounce) jars cheddar or pimiento cheese spread

Fig. 1   Fig. 2   Fig. 3

Preheat oven to 400°F. Open biscuit cans and separate biscuits. Stretch slightly, into ovals. For each shell, make deep cut marks at sides of base (fig. 1). Fan out dough to resemble a scallop shell (fig. 2). Cut six

slashes halfway through the fan (fig. 3). Place biscuits 3 inches apart on an ungreased baking sheet. Lightly brush with beaten egg and bake in an oven for 12 minutes or until golden brown. Cool. Split open and, just before serving, fill with tuna salad (or cheese spread).

KING TRITON'S TUNA SALAD

This flavorful recipe is a favorite with my kids, but if your children are very picky about exactly what goes in their tuna then definitely make it the way they like best.

Ingredients:

4 (6¹/2-ounce) cans solid white tuna (water-packed), drained
¹/3 cup chopped celery
¹/3 cup chopped scallions
1 tablespoon sweet pickle relish
³/4 teaspoon celery salt
¹/2 teaspoon onion powder
²/3 to ³/4 cup regular or reduced-fat mayonnaise
12 lettuce leaves

Combine tuna, celery, and scallions in a large mixing bowl. Stir relish, celery salt, and onion powder into mayonnaise. Add dressing to tuna and gently toss to combine. Chill until serving time. Serve in seashell biscuits on lettuce.
Preparation time: 20 minutes
Chilling time: 3 hours or overnight

Fruity Flounders

The Little Mermaid Party

Fig. 3

12 SERVINGS

Who isn't enchanted by Ariel's adorable little friend Flounder? Did you ever notice how much Flounder resembles a pear? Well, at this party, Flounder poses as a pear in a fresh fruit salad.

Ingredients:

8-ounce tub soft cream cheese
blue food coloring
12 lettuce leaves (Boston or red leaf)
12 premium quality (large) pear
  halves
12 miniature marshmallows
12 raisins
fresh dill (for garnish)

One hour before the party, blend cream cheese with food coloring to tint an even shade of deep blue. Fill a small pastry bag, fitted with a #4 round writing tip, and set aside for decorating the salad.

Arrange a lettuce leaf on each plate. Drain the pears and pat dry with paper towels. Place each pear half, cut-side down, on a lettuce leaf. Use pear slices to make tails and dorsal fins as shown (fig. 1). Cut a wedge out of the wide end of each pear for Flounder's mouth. Use the wedge to make a lower fin (fig. 2). Pipe cream cheese onto each pear in stripes to resemble Flounder, and press a marshmallow and a raisin into each pear to make an eye (fig. 3). Garnish with dill.

Preparation time: 35 minutes

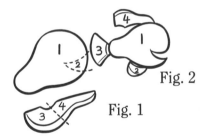

Fig. 2

Fig. 1

Guppy Cups

The Little Mermaid Party

12 SERVINGS

Poor Flounder! Whenever he was frightened, Ariel and the others would call him a guppy. Guppy Cups are decorated paper nut-cups filled with flavored, fish-shaped snack crackers.

Fig. 1

Ingredients:

1 envelope ranch-style salad dressing mix
1 teaspoon dried dill
1/4 cup melted butter or margarine
1 tablespoon olive oil
3 cups cheddar-flavored fish-shaped crackers
3 cups pretzel-flavored fish-shaped crackers
12 paper nut-cups (or soufflé cups) in white or pastel colors
colored felt-tip markers

Preheat oven to 250°F. Combine salad dressing mix, dill, butter, and oil in measuring cup and pour into the bottom of a 12" x 18" roasting pan. Scatter crackers over seasoning mixture in pan. Gently stir crackers until evenly coated. Bake crackers for 35 to 40 minutes, stirring every ten minutes. Be sure to store in airtight containers to ensure crispness. Crackers may be made up to one week in advance. Use felt-tip markers to draw fish, sea horses, and seaweed on cupcake liners. Place crackers in a glass fishbowl, and let kids fill their own guppy cups.
Preparation time: 12 minutes
Baking time: 35 to 40 minutes

Caribbean Blue Cooler

The Little Mermaid Party

Prepare a package of any powdered "blue" drink mix. Pour into ice cube trays and freeze. Serve ice cubes in glasses. Fill glasses using 4 liters of ginger ale.

Princess Pasta

Cinderella's Ball

12 SERVINGS

Spaghetti with meat sauce is a royal dish to every child, and a perfect partner to Breadstick Brooms (page 133). Being one of the most popular of all kid foods, why not serve it for all kinds of parties.

Ingredients:

2 pounds ground beef
2 tablespoons olive oil
2 cloves garlic, crushed
2 cups chopped onion
2 cups chopped green bell peppers
1 (16-ounce) can of tomato sauce
2 (16-ounce) cans of whole tomatoes,
*   undrained*
2 tablespoons chopped fresh (or 2
*   teaspoons dried) oregano leaves*
3 tablespoons chopped fresh (or 1
*   tablespoon dried) basil leaves*
1 teaspoon marjoram
1 teaspoon salt
1 tablespoon sugar (optional)
1/2 cup sliced ripe olives (optional)
8 cups cooked spaghetti
Parmesan cheese to taste

Brown ground beef in a large skillet and drain off fat. In a very large saucepan (about 3 quarts), sauté garlic, onion, and bell peppers until wilted. Add tomato sauce. Break up tomatoes and add to the sauce, along with the juice from the can. Stir in oregano, basil, marjoram, salt, sugar, olives, and drained beef. Bring to boil. Cover and simmer 1 hour. Serve over hot spaghetti with Parmesan cheese.
Preparation time: 20 minutes
Cooking time: 1 hour

*NO TIME? TIP: Use ready-made pasta sauce from jars and add to ground beef.

Royal Coach Wheels Primavera

Cinderella's Ball

12 SERVINGS

You can serve this dressed-up version of macaroni and cheese salad, right along-side the Princess Pasta (page 130) from your "Palace Pasta Bar."

Ingredients:

1 tablespoon olive oil
2 cups thinly sliced zucchini
1 cup thinly sliced pepperoni
1 1/3 cup regular or reduced-fat
*   mayonnaise*
2/3 cup buttermilk
1/3 cup fresh snipped chives
1/2 teaspoon salt
1/2 teaspoon black pepper
1 teaspoon onion powder
1 1/3 cups grated cheddar cheese
6 cups cooked rotelle (wheel) pasta,
*   well rinsed and drained*
1 (10-ounce) pkg. frozen peas,
*   thawed and drained*

In large saucepan, lightly sauté zucchini and pepperoni until zucchini is tender-crisp and pepperoni slices are lightly curled. Drain and set aside to cool. In a large mixing bowl, blend mayonnaise, buttermilk, chives, salt, pepper, and onion powder with wire whisk to make a smooth dressing. Stir in cheddar cheese. Add pasta, peas, and cooled zucchini with pepperoni. Gently toss. Cover salad and refrigerate 6 hours or overnight, to blend flavors.

Preparation time: 20 minutes
Chilling time: 6
hours or longer

Breadstick Brooms

Cinderella's Ball

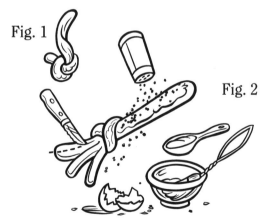

Fig. 1

Fig. 2

2 DOZEN

Poor Cinderella was always working—scrubbing, cooking, and sweeping. But these breadstick brooms are a delicious treat that have a magical way of disappearing.

Ingredients:

3 cans (8 count) refrigerated
*   breadsticks*
1 egg, slightly beaten
poppy seeds

Preheat oven to 350°F. Separate the breadsticks and unroll them, stretching to about 10 or 12 inches. Tie a knot in each stick, about 3 inches from one end. Cut four slits in each short end to resemble a tassel (fig. 1). Arrange the breadsticks about 3 inches apart on baking sheets coated with a nonstick cooking spray. Spread the tassels slightly. Brush the breadsticks with beaten egg and sprinkle the handles with poppy seeds (fig. 2). Bake 15 to 20 minutes.

Preparation time: 15 minutes
Baking time: 15 to 18 minutes

Glass Slipper Soda

Cinderella's Ball
Sleeping Beauty's Disney Princess Pizza Party

Wash an unused rubber shoe protector inside and out. Tape up heel opening with plastic tape. Fill with water and freeze. Unmold and float in a punch bowl filled with 4 liters of ginger ale tinted pink with 2/3 cup grenadine syrup.

Cheshire Cat Canapés

Happy Unbirthday Tea Party

1 DOZEN

Recruit your child's help in making these very expressive tea sandwiches.

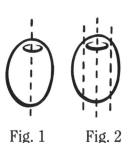

Fig. 1   Fig. 2   Fig. 3

Ingredients:

12 slices white bread
3 (5-ounce) jars of cheddar cheese spread, softened
12 pitted green olives (with or without pimiento stuffing)
12 pitted black olives
slivered almonds
2 slices of cheddar cheese
4-inch cookie cutter

Cut 4-inch circles out of bread with cookie cutter. Spread slices with cheese spread. Split green olives in half, lengthwise, so that they're oval-shaped (fig. 1). Shave off sides of olives so that they'll sit flat against the cheese (fig. 2). Cut black olives in half, lengthwise, and trim half of the halves into triangles like a cat's nose

133

(fig. 3). Arrange green olive slices on canapés for eyes and black olive triangles for noses. Cut slivers for pupils in the center of green olive eyes.

Cut almond slices in half and use to make "toothy grins" on canapés. Cut cheese slices into small triangles and use for ears (fig. 4). Place on tray and cover loosely with plastic wrap. Chill until serving time.
Preparation time: 30 minutes

Fig. 4

Queen of Hearts Card Canapés

Happy Unbirthday Tea Party

2 DOZEN

I find trying to make a whole set of cards a little confusing. To keep it simple, just choose the age of your child for the number and hearts for the suit.

Ingredients:

12 slices of white bread
2 (8-ounce) tubs cream cheese, at room temperature
gel or paste food-coloring (red)
small pastry bag fitted with coupling nozzle
#2 round writing tip

Trim crusts from bread and split each slice into two rectangles. Reserve 1/2 cup cream cheese, and spread the rest on bread. (If cream cheese doesn't spread very easily, beat with an electric mixer.) Tint reserved cream cheese red. Attach #2 round writing tip to small pastry bag and fill with red cream cheese. If your child is five, for example, pipe red cream cheese on canapés to look like "five of hearts" cards (five hearts and the number 5). It helps to use a real playing card as a model. Place canapés on a tray and cover loosely with plastic wrap. Chill until serving time.
Preparation time: 30 minutes

Marshmallow Magic Mushrooms

Happy Unbirthday Tea Party

6 DOZEN

These easy confections look like real mushrooms you can have for dessert. Kids love assembling them as an activity.

Ingredients:

2 (12-ounce) packages Nestlé Toll House Semi-Sweet Morsels
1/3 cup vegetable shortening
6 dozen vanilla wafers
6 dozen marshmallows
Nestlé Baking Cocoa (in a sugar shaker)

Melt chocolate and shortening in the top of a double boiler (or 1 to 2 1/2 minutes in the microwave). Stir until smooth.

Make mushrooms by dipping one end of a marshmallow into chocolate and sticking the flat bottom of a vanilla wafer on chocolate to resemble a mushroom cap. As soon as chocolate sets, shake cocoa on stems and caps to look like a dusting of soil.

Preparation time: 30 minutes

Tweedledum and Tweedledee Tea

Happy Unbirthday Tea Party

Prepare 1 gallon of unsweetened iced tea. Sweeten with two 6-ounce cans of frozen orange juice concentrate.

Belle's Baguettes (French Bread Pizza)

Beauty and the Beast Party and
Sleeping Beauty's Disney Princess Pizza Party

12 PIZZAS

Lorraine cheese, bacon, and sun-dried tomatoes on baguettes give these pizzas a French country flavor.

Ingredients:

1 (8-ounce) can tomato sauce
1 (6-ounce) can tomato paste
1 teaspoon Worcestershire sauce
1 clove crushed garlic
1 teaspoon dried, crushed rosemary
3 cups (12 ounces) grated Lorraine
    cheese
12 strips crisp cooked bacon, chopped
1/2 cup regular mayonnaise (do not
    substitute reduced fat or fat free in
    this recipe)
1 cup chopped sun-dried tomatoes,
    drained
3 (14") baguettes (French bread)

Preheat oven to 425°F. In small mixing bowl, combine tomato sauce, tomato paste, Worcestershire sauce, garlic, and rosemary. In a separate bowl, combine cheese, bacon, mayonnaise, and sun-dried tomatoes. Cut each loaf in half and split open so that you'll have twelve 7-inch slices. Arrange slices, cut side up, on baking sheet. Spread with tomato sauce mixture. Top with cheese mixture. Bake 10 to 15 minutes until golden and puffy. Serve hot.

Preparation time: 20 minutes
Baking time: 10 to 15 minutes

Lumiere's Candlestick Salad

Beauty and the Beast Party

12 SERVINGS

Candlestick salad is a classic that dates back to 1920's tea rooms. Children love it and so does Lumiere, who always serves it to Belle and the Beast.

Ingredients:

2 (3-ounce) packages cream
    cheese, softened
1 tablespoon apricot jam
2 tablespoons mayonnaise
6 bananas (as straight as possible)
12 fresh strawberries
12 canned pineapple rings, drained
12 lettuce leaves

Combine cream cheese and apricot jam in a mixing bowl and beat until smooth and creamy. Blend in mayonnaise. Just before serving, trim ends from bananas so that they are as straight as possible. Cut tops from strawberries. Arrange pineapple rings on lettuce leaves. Stand a banana upright in the center of each circle. Drizzle a spoonful of cheese mixture over the top and down the sides to resemble melted candle wax. Set a strawberry (cut-side down) on top of each banana, like a glowing flame. Serve immediately.

Preparation time:
10 minutes

Chip's Cherry Tea

Beauty and the Beast Party

Prepare 1 gallon of unsweetened iced tea. Add 2 tablespoons lemon juice and 1 cup grenadine syrup. Freeze ice cubes with maraschino cherries and serve in tea.

Prince Ali Kababwa Kabobs with Sultan's Sauce

Aladdin Party

12 SERVINGS

This exotic version of hot dogs is served with pita bread and Sultan's Sauce. Even finicky eaters get excited about trying these kebobs and the couscous that comes with it.

Ingredients:

12 extra-long franks
3 red bell peppers, cut in wedges
3 green bell peppers, cut in wedges
1 fresh or canned pineapple, cut into chunks
2 dozen cherry tomatoes
wooden skewers
olive oil
12 pita breads
Sultan's Sauce (recipe follows)

For each kabob: Slice a hot dog into 1-inch pieces. Thread onto skewer, alternating with red and green bell pepper wedges and pineapple chunks. Cover ends of kabobs with cherry tomatoes. Brush kabobs lightly with olive oil. Grill or broil until hot dogs are golden and peppers are browned but not charred, turning once or twice while cooking. (Depending on distance from heat source, this can take 6 to 10 minutes.) Serve with pita bread and Jasmine's Curried Couscous (below). If you prefer, you can pull skewers from kabobs before serving so that kids can roll them up in their pita bread. Pass Sultan's Sauce around on the side. This is particularly intriguing to kids when it's served from an Aladdin's lamplike sauce boat.

SULTAN'S SAUCE:

Ingredients:

1^{1}/3 cups regular or reduced-fat mayonnaise
^{1}/3 cup yellow mustard
1 tablespoon honey
^{1}/3 cup chopped mango chutney

Combine ingredients in a small mixing bowl and blend until smooth. Chill until serving time.
Preparation time: 15 minutes
Cooking time: 10 minutes

Jasmine's Curried Couscous

Aladdin Party

12 SERVINGS

Couscous is a staple on any Middle Eastern menu. This wheat grain semolina takes the place of pasta.

Ingredients:

^{1}/3 cup butter
1 tablespoon olive oil
^{1}/2 cup sliced almonds
^{1}/2 teaspoon salt
1 teaspoon curry powder
6 cups cooked couscous (prepared according to package directions)
^{1}/2 cup golden raisins
^{1}/3 cup fresh chopped parsley

Melt butter in a large skillet. Add olive oil and almonds. Sauté until almonds are golden. Stir in salt and curry powder. Toss with couscous, raisins, and parsley. Serve warm with kebobs.
Preparation time: 10 minutes
Cooking time: 10 minutes

Genie Guice

Aladdin Party

Combine 1/2 gallon of milk and 1/2 gallon of Concord grape juice.

Aladdin's Agrabah Market Ambrosia

Aladdin Party

12 SERVINGS

This fruit salad reflects the succulent selection from Agrabah market's produce stands, including the apple Jasmine "stole" from the angry vendor.

Ingredients:

2 tablespoons lime juice
3 tablespoons honey
1 tablespoon sugar
1 teaspoon cinnamon
3 apples
3 cups fresh pineapple chunks
2 (15-ounce) cans of mandarin
    orange sections, drained
1 cup pitted, chopped dates
1 cup shredded coconut

In a large mixing bowl, combine lime juice, honey, sugar, and cinnamon. Core apples (leaving peel on) and cut into cubes. Toss apple slices in bowl of lime juice mixture. (This will retard browning.) Add pineapple chunks, orange segments, dates, and half of coconut to the bowl. Toss gently to combine fruits. Cover and chill just an hour or two before serving. Spoon ambrosia into individual serving dishes or cups and sprinkle with remaining coconut.

Preparation time: 10 minutes
Chilling time: 1 to 2 hours

Rajah's Crispy Rice Tigers

Aladdin Party

12 TIGERS

These crisp cereal tigers will remind you of popcorn balls. Use them to decorate each child's place setting.

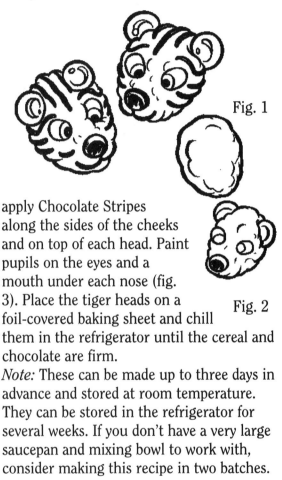

Fig. 1

Fig. 2

Ingredients:

6 tablespoons butter or margarine
orange gel food coloring (or a mixture of yellow and red)
8 cups miniature marshmallows
8 cups toasted rice cereal
2 dozen large orange gumdrops
2 dozen additional miniature marshmallows
1 dozen large black licorice gumdrops
Chocolate Stripes (recipe and instructions follow)

Melt the butter in a large saucepan and add 8 cups of marshmallows. Stir over low heat until the marshmallows melt and the mixture is smooth. Tint the mixture bright orange with the food coloring. Remove the pan from the heat. Place cereal in a large bowl and add marshmallow mixture. Gently stir until it's evenly coated. Allow to cool for about three minutes. With buttered hands, divide the mixture into a dozen egg-shaped balls (fig. 1). Flatten the orange gumdrops with your fingers, and press one into each side of the end of an oval for ears. Press two miniature marshmallows into each head for eyes, and press a black gumdrop into the small end of each head for the nose (fig. 2). Using a clean, narrow-pointed paintbrush,

apply Chocolate Stripes along the sides of the cheeks and on top of each head. Paint pupils on the eyes and a mouth under each nose (fig. 3). Place the tiger heads on a foil-covered baking sheet and chill them in the refrigerator until the cereal and chocolate are firm.

Note: These can be made up to three days in advance and stored at room temperature. They can be stored in the refrigerator for several weeks. If you don't have a very large saucepan and mixing bowl to work with, consider making this recipe in two batches.

CHOCOLATE STRIPES:

Ingredients:

2 tablespoons shortening
1 (6-ounce) bag Nestlé Toll House Semi-Sweet Morsels

Melt the chips and shortening in the top of a double boiler (or in a microwave). Stir until smooth.

Preparation time: 45 minutes
Chilling time: 30 minutes or longer

140

Popcorn Cobras

Aladdin Party

12 COBRAS

Candied popcorn is wrapped in green cellophane to make a slinky snake. This python even has a red ribbon tongue!

Materials:

2 rolls green cellophane
8 quarts popcorn (caramel, green apple, or any variety of flavors from a popcorn shop)
curling ribbon (yellow and red)
4 (9" x 12") sheets green construction paper
1 (8" x 11") sheet white paper
glue
scissors
black felt-tip marker

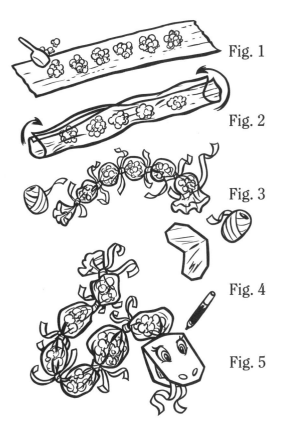

Fig. 1

Fig. 2

Fig. 3

Fig. 4

Fig. 5

You can make these yourself as a party favor, or turn it into a get-acquainted activity. Have bowls of assorted popcorn set out on a table along with the craft materials. (It's a good idea to precut the python heads from the construction paper and to have a sample snake already made up.) For each python head, fold construction paper in half lengthwise and cut into thirds. Cut 1-inch slash lengthwise along center of each crease. Trim corners at opposite end to create nose. Set python heads aside. Tear off 6 inches of cellophane. Show children how to place about 1/4 cup of popcorn at 4-inch intervals down the length of the cellophane (fig. 1), leaving about 6 inches at each end. Roll up the plastic in a tube around the popcorn (fig. 2). Tie off into sections using short pieces of yellow ribbon (fig. 3). Pull one end of the cellophane through slash in the crease of python head. Tie a knot in the cellophane so it won't slip back through the slash (fig. 4). Tie a 12-inch strand of red ribbon around knot in the mouth for a tongue. Cut out eyes from white paper, glue them on, and draw pupils and nostrils on the head with a marker (fig. 5).

Preparation time: 5 minutes per cobra

Pizza Planet's Buzz Burger Pizza

Toy Story Party

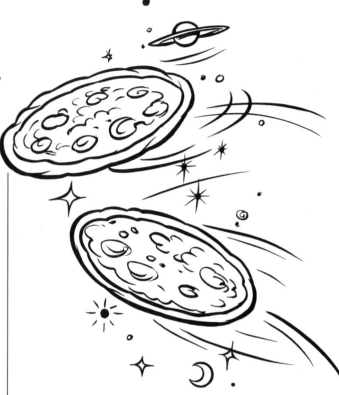

TWO 12-INCH PIZZAS

Pizza meets cheeseburger makes this a match made in heaven for kids. This easy pat-in-the-pan crust is almost as easy as calling the Pizza Planet delivery truck!

Ingredients:

1 lb. hamburger
1 1/2 cups tomato sauce
1/3 cup tomato paste
2 cloves crushed garlic
2 teaspoons Italian seasoning
1 small red onion
2 cups (8 ounces) grated mozzarella
  cheese
1 cup (4 ounces) grated cheddar
  cheese
1/4 cup (1 ounce) grated Parmesan
  cheese
2 12-inch Pizza Planet Crusts
  (next page)

Adjust oven rack to lowest position. Preheat oven to 425°F. Brown hamburger in a large skillet and drain. Mix tomato sauce, tomato paste, garlic, and Italian seasoning in a small bowl or glass measuring cup. Thinly slice onion and separate slices. Assemble pizzas: Spread half of sauce over each prepared crust. Divide hamburger evenly between both crusts.

Sprinkle 1 cup of mozzarella over each pizza. Divide onion slices between pizzas. Top each pizza with half of the cheddar and Parmesan cheeses. Bake each pizza 15 to 20 minutes, or until crust is golden brown. Serve hot.
Preparation time: 25 minutes
Baking time: 15 to 20 minutes

*NO TIME? TIP: Use refrigerated, canned pizza dough for crusts, substitute ready-made pizza sauce in recipe.

Woody's Wild Western Wiener Pizza

Toy Story Party

TWO 12-INCH PIZZAS

This unconventional western-style pizza features barbecue sauce and franks.

Ingredients:

1 (16-ounce) package (10) franks
1 cup chopped red bell pepper
1 cup chopped green bell pepper
2 cups barbecue sauce
2 cups (12 ounces) grated Monterey
   Jack or cheddar cheese
2 (12") Pizza Planet Crusts (right)

Adjust oven rack to lowest position. Preheat oven to 425°F. Cut franks into half-inch-thick slices. Spread each prepared crust with half of barbecue sauce. Divide franks and peppers evenly between both crusts. Top each pizza with half of cheese. Bake each pizza 15 to 20 minutes, or until crust is golden brown. Serve hot.
Preparation time: 15 minutes
Baking time: 15 to 20 minutes

NO TIME? TIP: Use refrigerated, canned pizza dough for crusts.

PIZZA PLANET CRUST
4 12-INCH CRUSTS

Ingredients:

2 packages dry active yeast
2 cups warm water (105°F–115°F)
1 tablespoon honey
1/4 cup olive oil
2 teaspoons salt
5 cups all-purpose flour
shortening
cornmeal

Dissolve yeast in warm water in a medium-size bowl. Stir in honey, olive oil, and salt. Blend in flour. Divide dough into four equal-size balls. Grease four 12-inch pizza pans with shortening and dust with cornmeal so that the surface is coated. With floured hands, flatten each ball of dough. Pull and stretch into 12-inch circles. Pat into prepared pans.
Preparation time: 20 minutes

Space Slaw

Toy Story Party

12 SERVINGS

O.K.…You've got to serve some kind of vegetable with pizza. This space slaw comes with every order at Pizza Planet.

Ingredients:

1/2 cup sour cream or yogurt
3/4 cup regular or reduced-fat
 mayonnaise
1 teaspoon sugar
1/2 teaspoon salt
1/2 teaspoon dry mustard
2 tablespoons onion powder
1 tablespoon fresh or (1 teaspoon
 dried) dill
6 cups shredded green cabbage
1 cup shredded carrots

In a large mixing bowl, combine sour cream, mayonnaise, sugar, salt, mustard, onion powder, and dill. Blend until smooth. Toss in cabbage and carrots. Cover and chill at least 3 hours for flavors to blend.
Preparation time: 5 minutes
Chilling time: 3 hours or longer

Pizza Planet Popcorn Aliens

Toy Story Party

12 POPCORN BALLS

Remember those "charming" little creatures in Pizza Planet's claw machine (the ones with three eyes) that kept Buzz Lightyear company? Here's how to make the popcorn version.

Ingredients:

3/4 cup sugar
6 tablespoons butter or margarine
3/4 cup light corn syrup
1/4 teaspoon salt
gel or paste food-coloring (green)
12 cups of popped popcorn
3 dozen Life Saver Candies
1 cup Nestlé Toll House
  Semi-Sweet Morsels
12 small red gumdrops, flattened
  with rolling pin
12 Tootsie Roll Pops
plastic wrap

Combine sugar, margarine, and corn syrup in a Dutch oven or heavy-duty 6-quart saucepan. Tint to desired shade of green with food-coloring. Bring to a boil and stir two minutes. Remove from heat and stir in popcorn. Cover a baking sheet with foil. Dip hands in cold water and shape into 2½-inch balls. Place on foil. While slightly warm, press three LifeSavers into each ball for eyes and use chocolate morsels for pupils. Use gumdrops for tongues and press pops into heads for antennas. When completely cool, wrap in plastic wrap.
Preparation time: 30 minutes
Cooking time: 2 minutes

Flying Saucer Soda

Toy Story Party

Cut slashes in fruit-flavored gumdrops and hang on the edges around drinking cups. Fill with soda and serve with long plastic straws.

Pocahontas Wild Turkey Pyes

Pocahontas Party

2 DOZEN

If your kids are big hamburger fans, you can always substitute ground beef for turkey. This recipe is large enough to serve a party of twelve children two "pyes" (colonial spelling of pie) each. If you have a smaller party or only want to serve one pye per guest, cut the recipe in half.

145

Ingredients:

2 (10-ounce) cans (10 count) and 1
    (5-ounce) can (5 count) of
    refrigerated buttermilk biscuits
3 to 4 tablespoons yellow cornmeal
2 pounds ground turkey
1 cup chopped onions
1 cup chopped celery
1 cup chopped green pepper
1 teaspoon poultry seasoning
1 12-ounce bottle of chili sauce
24 canned baby corn ears, drained
2 cups (8 ounces) grated cheddar
    cheese

Preheat oven to 375°F. Grease 24 muffin cups and dust with cornmeal so that the bottoms and sides are thoroughly coated. Turn upside down and shake out any excess cornmeal. Separate biscuits (you'll have one spare) and flatten into 5-inch circles. Line each muffin cup with a biscuit, pressing against bottom and sides. Chill while preparing meat. Brown ground turkey, onion, celery, and green pepper in a large skillet until meat is cooked and vegetables are tender. Drain off any excess fat. Stir in poultry seasoning and chili sauce. Divide filling equally among biscuit cups. Place a corn cob on top of each biscuit and sprinkle with cheese. Bake 18 to 20 minutes, or until golden brown. Serve hot.
Preparation time: 20 minutes
Baking time: 18 to 20 minutes

Indian Corn

Pocahontas Party

12 SERVINGS

Chili powder adds color to otherwise ordinary corn on the cob.

Ingredients:

12 ears fresh or frozen corn
1/2 cup butter or margarine
1 teaspoon chili powder
1 teaspoon paprika

Bring a large kettle of water to a boil. Add corn and return to boil. Cook 6 to 8 minutes or until tender. Melt butter, chili powder, and paprika together. Brush over corn ears before serving.
Preparation time:
5 minutes
Cooking time:
6 to 8 minutes

Grandmother Willow Tree Tea

Pocahontas Party

Prepare 1 gallon of unsweetened iced tea. Sweeten with two 6-ounce cans of frozen apple juice concentrate.

Jasmine's Pineapple Pita Pizza

Sleeping Beauty's Disney Princess Pizza Party

12 PIZZAS

Ingredients:

1 (12-ounce) bottle chili sauce
1 teaspoon curry powder
1 cup chopped green pepper
1 cup (4 ounces) grated cheddar cheese
1 cup (4 ounces) grated Swiss cheese
8 pineapple rings, drained
6 pita breads

Preheat oven to 425°F. Combine chili sauce and curry powder in small mixing bowl. In another bowl, toss chopped pepper and grated cheeses together. Split open pita bread so that each one gives you two pizza shells. Arrange shells on baking sheets. Spread with chili sauce. Divide pepper and cheese mixture evenly among pita shells and top each one with a pineapple slice. Bake 10 to 15 minutes, or until cheese is bubbling and pineapple is glazed. Serve hot.
Preparation time: 15 minutes
Baking time: 10 to 15 minutes

Pocahontas Pizza

Sleeping Beauty's Disney Princess Pizza Party

12 PIZZAS

Inspired by Native American cuisine, these pizzas feature a cornmeal crust.

Ingredients:

1¼ cups mild salsa
2 tablespoons tomato paste
12 ounces smoked turkey, sliced
1 pound can baby corn ears
2 cups grated white cheddar cheese
12 tostada shells

Preheat oven to 400°F. Combine salsa and tomato paste in small mixing bowl. Cut turkey into julienne strips. Split baby corn ears in half. Arrange tostada shells on baking sheets and spread with salsa sauce mix.

Divide turkey and corn ears evenly among tostadas and top with cheese. Place on baking sheets and bake for 8 to 14 minutes, or until cheese is bubbling. (Do not allow tostadas to burn.)

Preparation time: 10 minutes
Baking time: 8 to 14 minutes

Enchanted Hot Chocolate

Sleeping Beauty's Disney Princess Pizza Party

Prepare 1 gallon of hot cocoa mix with milk. Add 2 tablespoons cinnamon. Serve in mugs with miniature marshmallows and whole cinnamon sticks.

Peanut Butter Popcorn Palace

Sleeping Beauty's Disney Princess Pizza Party

12+ SERVINGS

Popcorn and slumber parties just seem to go together. Guests at this party gather in the kitchen to mold gooey globs of popcorn into a massive edible edifice that's fun to eat! Divide so that there are three groups of four kids each, mixing up the recipe. Everyone joins together to create the towers and build the complete palace.

For each batch, melt 1 cup of peanut butter with one package of butterscotch morsels in the top of a double boiler (or in a microwave). Stir the mixture until it's smooth, then pour it over a bowl filled with 10 cups of popcorn. Let the kids mix the popcorn and the mixture together until the popcorn is evenly coated. Begin the construction of the palace by using the first batch of popcorn as the base and the second and third batches as walls and towers.

Top the towers with ice-cream cones. Decorate the walls with chocolate candies for battlements. Pieces of the chocolate bars serve as doors, windows, and the drawbridge.

Preparation time: 30 minutes

Ingredients:

3 cups smooth-style peanut butter
3 (12-ounce) packages Nestlé
*   Toll House butterscotch morsels*
30 cups of popcorn (about 2 gallons)
chocolate-flavored ice-cream cones
2 Nestlé Crunch chocolate bars,
*   broken in pieces*
4 to 6 (1.55-ounce) Nestlé Milk
*   Chocolate Candy Bars*
20-inch square cake board (or foil-
*   covered cardboard)*

Hunchback Honey Glazed "Pigeon Wings"

Hunchback of Notre Dame Party

12 SERVINGS

In cities throughout the world, pigeons are naturally attracted to statues. The gargoyles of Notre Dame were no exception. Poor Laverne was so tormented by roosting pigeons, she would have thought that roasting them was a good idea! For this recipe, however, we'll use chicken wings.

Ingredients:

1¹/₂ cups orange juice
¹/₃ cup honey
¹/₃ cup red wine vinegar
¹/₂ teaspoon dry mustard
¹/₂ teaspoon ginger
2 tablespoons Worcestershire sauce
1 tablespoon olive oil
1 to 2 cloves crushed garlic
3 dozen chicken wings, disjointed
Honey Glaze (recipe follows)

Preheat oven to 375°F. Combine orange juice, honey, red wine vinegar, vinegar mustard, ginger, Worcestershire sauce, olive oil, and garlic in a large glass measuring cup. Arrange chicken in one or two casserole dishes. Pour marinade over chicken. Cover and refrigerate for 4 to 8 hours.

Cover the bottom of a broiler pan with foil. Place rack over foil and arrange as many chicken wings as you can on rack without overcrowding. (You may have to do these in two batches.) Bake wings for 30 minutes, turning once. Brush with some glaze and bake 10 to 15 minutes longer until very golden but not burned. Serve hot with remaining glaze as a dipping sauce.

HONEY GLAZE:

1¹/₂ cups honey
1 cup apricot preserves
¹/₄ cup red wine vinegar
2 teaspoons Worcestershire sauce
1 teaspoon dry mustard
2 teaspoons grated orange peel

Combine honey, apricot preserves, vinegar, Worcestershire sauce, dry mustard, and orange peel in a saucepan. Bring to a boil. Reduce heat and simmer 1 minute. Cool to room temperature.
Preparation time: 20 minutes
Marinating time: 4 to 8 hours
Cooking time: 40 to 45 minutes

NO TIME? TIP: Buy take-out buffalo wings or frozen fried chicken wings.

Phoebus Phries with Bell Tower Tomato Sauce

Hunchback of Notre Dame Party

12 SERVINGS

These easy, oven-baked fries have a French accent. Dijon mustard and dill give common ketchup a Parisian twist. In this recipe, do not substitute fat-free mayonnaise for regular mayonnaise. Because these potatoes are not actually fried, they need some oil to baste them while baking.

Ingredients:

6 large baking potatoes
³/4 cup regular mayonnaise
salt
Bell Tower Tomato Sauce
    (recipe follows)

Preheat oven to 400°F. Peel potatoes and cut into half-inch sticks. Divide potatoes into three parts. Spoon ¼ cup of mayonnaise into a gallon-size plastic bag. Add one batch of potatoes and shake to coat evenly. Arrange in a single layer on a jelly-roll pan,

coated with nonstick cooking spray. (Potatoes should not touch.) Repeat the same procedure with remaining two batches of potatoes and mayonnaise. Sprinkle lightly with salt. Bake one tray at a time, turning once with spatula, 20 to 30 minutes, or until golden brown and crisp. (As soon as all of the potatoes have been baked, you can combine them in one pan to keep them warm in the oven.)

BELL TOWER TOMATO SAUCE:

Ingredients:

2 cups chili sauce
1 cup ketchup
¹/4 cup Dijon-style mustard
1 tablespoon fresh (or 1 teaspoon dried) dill weed

Combine the above ingredients in a bowl or 1-quart glass measuring cup. Cover with plastic wrap and allow flavors to blend in the refrigerator overnight. Kids like to use this sauce with their fries, so allow ¼ cup per child. Serve in paper soufflé cups.

*NO TIME? TIP: You can always substitute frozen steak fries for this hand-cut variety and serve them with the Bell Tower Tomato Sauce.

Esmeralda's Ruby and Emerald Grapes with Cheese Balls and Baguettes

Hunchback of Notre Dame Party

12 SERVINGS

Fruit and cheese is a classic course with any French meal. These are served in individual wooden salad bowls with breadsticks, perfect pick-up food for little fingers.

Ingredients:

1 pound Bel Paese cheese or white American cheese (unsliced)
2/3 cup toasted, chopped almonds
1 pound seedless green grapes
1 pound seedless red grapes
packaged breadsticks (allow 2 to 3 per child)

Allow cheese to soften to room temperature. Divide into three dozen cubes of equal size. Roll cheese into balls, using your fingers. Place chopped almonds in a shallow pan. Roll cheese balls in almonds until completely coated. Place on a tray, cover with plastic wrap, and chill until serving time. Arrange clusters of green and red grapes in small wooden salad bowls. Add three cheese balls to each bowl. Insert breadsticks at an angle, nestling them between a bunch of grapes. (You may have to break very long breadsticks in half.)

Preparation time: 15 minutes
Chilling time: 1 hour or longer

Quasimodo Quencher

Hunchback of Notre Dame Party

Fill glasses halfway up using 1/2 gallon of white grape juice. Fill the rest of the way using 2 liters of ginger ale.

152

Herc's Hero Gyros

Hercules Party

12 SERVINGS

These are really just hellenized hamburgers. Although authentic gyros are made with lamb, most children prefer ground beef or turkey.

Ingredients:

3 pounds ground beef, turkey, or lamb
3/4 cup finely chopped onion
1/3 cup lemon juice
3 tablespoons tomato paste
3 to 4 cloves of crushed garlic
2 teaspoons ground cumin
2 teaspoons dried oregano
1 teaspoon salt
1/2 teaspoon pepper
nonstick olive oil cooking spray
12 six-inch pitas
6 cups shredded iceberg or romaine lettuce
4 medium tomatoes, chopped and drained
Pegasus Sauce (recipe follows)

In a large mixing bowl, combine ground meat and onion. Mix lemon juice, tomato paste, garlic, and dry seasonings in a separate dish and stir into ground meat. Divide meat mixture into twelve balls of equal size. Flatten each patty as thin as you can between two sheets of waxed paper. Place patties in the freezer for about half an hour before grilling. (This makes thin patties easier to handle.) Coat a nonstick griddle or skillet with cooking spray. Grill patties over medium heat, turning several times until juices run clear (about 10 to 12 minutes). You may need to cook these in several batches and keep them warm on a baking sheet in the oven. In fact, these patties can be cooked a day in advance and reheated in the oven.

To assemble gyros: Split each pita bread halfway around the edge. Slip gyro patties into pita bread and top with lettuce, tomato, and Pegasus Sauce.

PEGASUS SAUCE:

Ingredients:
2 cups plain yogurt
3 tablespoons chopped fresh dill (or 3 teaspoons dried)
1 tablespoon sugar
1/4 teaspoon salt
1 cup seeded, diced cucumber

Combine yogurt, dill, sugar, salt, and cucumber in a mixing bowl. Chill several hours or overnight to blend flavors.
Preparation time: 20 minutes
Cooking time: 20 to 30 minutes

Note: If children prefer, they can top their gyros with ketchup or mustard.

153

Megara's Muffulettas

Hercules Party

12 SERVINGS

This famous sandwich has several variations, but it usually features traditional Greek olives. If using the genuine article, be sure to cut out all of the pits!

Ingredients:

2 large round loaves of Italian bread (8- or 10-inch)
1 pound thinly sliced salami
12 ounces thinly sliced provolone cheese
1/2 pound thinly sliced baked ham
Olive Salad (recipe follows)

Split each loaf of bread in half, horizontally. Hollow out halves so that only a half inch of soft bread remains against the crust, forming four shells. Drain Olive Salad and reserve marinade. Brush marinade over inside surface of bread shells. In two of "bottoms," layer as follows: salami, Olive Salad, provolone cheese, and Olive Salad. Cover each with a "top," wrap in plastic wrap, and refrigerate. After chilling at least four hours (or overnight), unwrap and cut each loaf into six wedges, just prior to serving.

OLIVE SALAD:

Ingredients:

2/3 cup olive oil
2 tablespoons lemon juice
2 cloves crushed garlic
1/4 cup minced parsley
1 tablespoon Worcestershire sauce
1 teaspoon dried oregano
1 cup chopped pimiento, well drained
1 1/2 cups chopped Greek olives (or black olives)
1/2 cup chopped bread-and-butter pickles

Blend olive oil, lemon juice, garlic, parsley, Worcestershire sauce, and oregano in a mixing bowl. Stir in olives, pimientos, and pickles. Cover and refrigerate overnight to blend flavors.
Preparation time: 25 minutes
Chilling time: Overnight

Phil's Phyllo Pie

Hercules Party

12 SERVINGS

Since Philoctetes was a satyr (half man, half grumpy old goat) it seems appropriate that his favorite training table meal would feature feta, a Greek goat cheese.

Ingredients:

2 ten-ounce packages frozen spinach, thawed and squeezed dry
12 ounces feta cheese crumbled (about 2 cups)*
1/2 cup finely chopped onion
2 tablespoons minced parsley
2 tablespoons fresh minced dill (or 2 teaspoons dried dill)
1/2 teaspoon salt
3 eggs, beaten
2 teaspoons olive oil
1/2 cup butter or margarine, melted
20 sheets of frozen phyllo dough, thawed (about half of a 16-ounce package)

*If you fear your child and guests won't like the strong taste of feta, substitute 12 ounces of ricotta cheese, or mix equal parts of both feta and ricotta.

Preheat oven to 350°F and grease a 9-by-13-inch baking dish with olive oil.

In a large mixing bowl, combine spinach, cheese, onion, parsley, dill, salt, and eggs. Fold the first sheet of phyllo dough into the baking dish, so that it fits edge to edge. Brush with melted butter. Repeat with nine more sheets. Cover with spinach filling. Cover filling with remaining ten sheets of phyllo dough, using the same butter layering method as before.

Score the top layer of pastry with a sharp knife to mark twelve portions. Bake, uncovered, for 30 to 35 minutes, or until golden brown. Let stand 10 minutes. Cut through scored lines and serve.

Note: When working with phyllo sheets, handle them carefully as you separate them, and always keep unused sheets covered with a damp towel to prevent them from drying out.

Preparation time: 20 minutes
Baking time: 30 to 35 minutes

Cyclops Potatoes

Hercules Party

12 SERVINGS

These petite baked potatoes are very amusing to kids. Add sour cream, olives, and a child's imagination and they look just like "Cyclops's eyes!"

Ingredients:

12 medium-size new potatoes
2 tablespoons regular or garlic-flavored olive oil
1 cup sour cream
12 pitted black olives

Preheat oven to 400°F.

Wash potatoes and pat dry. Split each potato in half.

Brush 1 tablespoon of oil on the bottom of a 10-by-15-inch baking pan. Arrange potatoes, cut-side down, and brush with remaining olive oil.

Bake for about 30 to 35 minutes, or until potatoes are golden and tender. Serve potatoes, cut-side up, on a platter. Garnish each potato in the center with a spoonful of sour cream. For the "pupil" of each "eye," split a ripe olive in half, lengthwise. Position olive halves, cut-side down, in the center of the sour cream.

Preparation time: 10 minutes
Baking time: 30 to 35 minutes

Athenian Ambrosia Almond Crunch

Hercules Party

12 SERVINGS

You could call this granola snack "junk food fit for the gods." It's made with lots of heavenly tasting healthy stuff like honey-roasted almonds and, of course, coconut! As every god and goddess knows, you can't have authentic ambrosia without it.

Ingredients:

1 twelve-ounce box of granola
1 four-ounce can of honey-roasted almonds
1 cup shredded coconut
1 cup pitted, chopped dates
1 cup golden raisins

Combine granola, almonds, coconut, dates, and raisins in a large mixing bowl. Serve in several small wooden salad bowls.

Preparation time: 5 minutes

Herculade and Zeus Juice

Hercules

Cover juice boxes with labels you and your child customize. Simply cut strips of construction paper wide enough to wrap around juice boxes. With crayons, create HERCULADE labels for one flavor, and ZEUS JUICE for another. Or you can avoid any controversy by serving the same flavor of juice under different labels.

Let Them Eat Cake

The cake is the climax of a birthday, the pinnacle of the party, the focus of the fantasy theme. What it isn't, or shouldn't be, is intimidating to make. You do not need special cake pans to make any of the cakes in this book. An industry has evolved around novelty pans but these really aren't required. All you need are basic pans: 8", 9", or 10" round, 8" or 9" square, 13" x 9" rectangular, 12-cup bundt, 9" x 5" loaf pans, and muffin pans for cupcakes. You can create just about any shape imaginable by cutting these cakes and rearranging their pieces into edible sculptures. You can even bake dome-shaped cakes in bowls or custard cups. This is a fun art form, once you are familiar with it.

Party Cake Pointers

When it comes to cake decorating, your tools make all the difference between breezing through a recipe or dealing with a disaster. Although it's not essential, I always emphasize the use of *baking parchment*. It just makes everything so much easier. Cut it to fit any flat bottomed cake pan, and you can eliminate greasing and flouring the pan. When the cake has cooled, simply peel the paper off the back . . . no surprises, no broken cakes. Of course, when baking in bundt, tube, or contour bottom pans, you can't use baking parchment. In these situations you must grease and flour the pan, so here are two tips:

1. *Always use a generous layer of solid vegetable shortening. Butter or margarine can stick because they contain water and salt.*
2. *Spoon about 3 tablespoons of flour in average-size pans and shake it around until the greased surface is evenly coated. Turn pan upside down and tap out all excess flour.*

Cooling racks are also important. You should have several so that you can invert cakes, then put another rack on top to flip them right-side up. Rubber spatulas are a must to scrape up every last drop of batter or frosting (if your child doesn't beat you to it!). They are also useful for folding in ingredients and filling pastry bags. Metal spatulas are the best tools for spreading and smoothing frostings. I find the angled ones are easiest to use and would never be without at least one large and one small one.

You should also invest in assorted sizes of pastry bags, coupling nozzles, and decorating tips. I'm not talking about expensive premade sets. I've compiled a list of the most useful ones. These can be used for decorating all kinds of food. After a while, you'll wonder how you ever lived without them.

Remember when you bake a cake, that you'll need something to serve it on. Party cakes are odd shapes and often arranged in expansive dimensions. Ready-cut, foil-bonded cake boards come in many sizes. However, I find it less expensive (and more flexible) to cut my own out of cardboard. Cover the boards with regular aluminum or colored foil.

To color frostings, you should always use gel- or paste-style food-colorings. These come in a wide assortment of shades and a little bit goes a long way (they're very vibrant). Best of all, they won't thin down your frosting. Of the two types, I prefer buying gels whenever possible. The cleanup of pastry bags (and your hands) seems much easier.

Although you can buy all of these supplies at gourmet cookware and cake decorating shops, gone are the days when you had to hunt for a source. I can find these materials in department stores, discount stores, supermarkets, even some drugstores.

Party Cake Tools

Pans:
   8", 9", and 10" round
   8" and 9" square
   13" x 9" rectangular
   12-cup bundt pan
   9" x 5" loaf pans
   muffin pan (for cupcakes)

Baking Parchment: Available in sheets or rolls, individual liners for cupcakes

Wire Cake Racks: 3 or 4

Rubber Spatulas: These are indispensable for scraping batter and frosting bowls. Buy a set of assorted sizes.

Metal Spatulas: Have at least one large- and one small-angled spatula for spreading and smoothing frostings.

Pastry Bags: You should look for reusable plastic-coated bags in 8", 12", and 18" or 20" lengths. Disposable bags are convenient for small amounts of frosting. These are useful for all kinds of food decorating, including ice-cream desserts.

Coupling Nozzles: These allow you to use decorating tips interchangeably.

Round Tips: #2, #3, #4 (small); #10 or #12 (medium); #5 or #6 (large)

Star Tips: #18, #24 (small); #5 (medium); #4B, #8B (large)

Leaf Tips: #66 or #67

Ribbon Tip: #47 (large); #48 (medium)

Gel or Paste Food-Coloring: These will not thin frosting.

Cake Boards or Foil-Covered Cardboard: Size specified for cake.

Basic Batters

Most of the cake recipes in this book are from scratch, using a one-bowl method for mixing convenience. However, if you're pinched for time, do not hesitate to use a cake mix instead. There's no shame in taking shortcuts. In fact, with more complicated cake constructions, I actually recommend using a mix to save time.

In addition to special flavor batters, I've included basic batters that can be used interchangeably to create just about any cake your child desires. Remember that pan sizes will vary according to the shape of cake and baking times will vary according to pan size. Just like standard cake mixes (which you can also use), these recipes yield enough batter for: one 13" x 9" pan, two 9" round pans, two or three 8" round pans, two 9" x 5" loaf pans, one 9" square pan and one 8" round pan, two 8" square pans, one 12-cup bundt pan, or two dozen cupcakes. Oven temperatures vary with pans, so refer to the temperature and time chart. (*Note*:

Allow at least a 2-inch space between pans when baking them in the same oven. This reduces their "natural attraction" to each other, which always results in lopsided cakes.) Cakes are done when a toothpick in the center comes out clean. Cakes should cool 10 minutes before inverting onto wire racks. As soon as they're turned out of the pans, immediately use a second rack to invert back into the upright position. (This is important because a cake that is very rounded on top can split in half when turned upside down.) Always level off the top of a cake when completely cool, using a serrated knife.

Temperature and Timetable

Note: When baking in glass pans, temperature is usually 325°F. Pan sizes are geared to the volume of batter yielded from Basic Yellow Butter Cake (next page), Basic Dutch Chocolate Cake (next page), or a standard packaged cake mix.

PAN SIZES	OVEN TEMP	BAKING TIME
9" x 13" (one)	350°F	35–40 minutes
9" round (two)	350°F	30–35 minutes
8" round (two)	325°F	35–40 minutes
8" round (three)	325°F	30–35 minutes
9" square and 8" round	325°F	35–40 minutes
9" square (two)	350°F	30–35 minutes
8" square (two)	325°F	35–40 minutes
9" x 5" loaf pans (two)	325°F	30–35 minutes
12-cup bundt pan (one)	325°F	45–50 minutes
24 cupcakes	325°F	25–30 minutes

BASIC YELLOW BUTTER CAKE

12 SERVINGS

Ingredients:
2 cups all-purpose flour
$1^1/2$ cups sugar
$1/4$ cup shortening, softened
$1/4$ cup ($1/2$ stick) butter or margarine, softened
1 cup milk
$3^1/2$ teaspoons baking powder
1 teaspoon salt
2 teaspoons vanilla extract
3 eggs

Preheat oven according to pan size (refer to specific recipe or Temperature and Timetable). Grease and flour pan(s) or line with baking parchment. Combine all ingredients in a large mixing bowl. Beat at medium speed for 30 seconds, scraping bowl constantly until blended. Beat on high speed for three minutes, scraping bowl occasionally. Pour into prepared pan(s) and bake for the required amount of time, or until a toothpick inserted in the center comes out clean. Cool on wire rack(s) ten minutes. Invert from pan(s) and cool completely. (If using parchment, peel away paper.)
Preparation time: 15 minutes
Baking time: refer to Temperature and Timetable (page 161)

BASIC DUTCH CHOCOLATE CAKE

12 SERVINGS

Dutch-processed cocoa is darker and richer than ordinary cocoa and gives this batter a fudgy flavor.

Ingredients:
$1^2/3$ cups all-purpose flour
1 cup sugar
$1/2$ cup firmly packed brown sugar
$2/3$ cup Nestlé Baking Cocoa
$1/4$ cup shortening, softened
$1/4$ cup ($1/2$ stick) butter or
   margarine, softened
$1^1/2$ cups buttermilk
$1^1/2$ teaspoons baking soda
1 teaspoon salt
2 teaspoons vanilla extract
2 eggs

Preheat oven according to pan size (refer to specific recipe or Temperature and Timetable). Grease and flour pan(s) or line with baking parchment. Combine all ingredients in a large mixing bowl. Beat at medium speed for 30 seconds, scraping bowl constantly until blended. Beat on high speed for three minutes, scraping bowl occasionally. Pour into prepared pan(s) and bake for the required amount of time, or until a toothpick inserted in the center comes out clean. Cool on wire rack(s) ten minutes. Invert from pan(s) and cool completely. (If using parchment, peel away paper.)
Preparation time: 15 minutes
Baking time: refer to Temperature and Timetable (page 161)

Freezing Cakes

If budgeting your time means planning ahead, consider baking your cake several weeks in advance and freezing it. It's possible to freeze finished, decorated cakes—but there's no guarantee what will happen when they defrost. Food colors have a funny way of bleeding into each other when they return from subzero to room temperature. So, I recommend freezing undecorated freshly baked cakes, which should be cooled completely, then wrapped tightly in plastic wrap. Freezing cakes actually makes them easier to cut into special shapes. If you know you'll be freezing your cakes, wait to level off the tops until you're ready to use them.

Basic Frostings: Tips and Techniques

Nothing can compare with the flavor of homemade frosting. Let's face it, some commercial products taste like cold cream. Even if you've baked your cake from a mix, no one will suspect it if you cover it with homemade frosting. If you must invest time in anything, make the frosting from scratch! It's also more economical. The average can of frosting contains about 1½ cups. The average party cake needs 2½ to 5 cups of frosting for ample coverage. The recipes in this book never skimp on this subject. Besides, isn't one of childhood's greatest joys spare frosting from your very own birthday cake? I always begged my mom to let me lick the bowl.

With the exception of certain customized frostings for specific cakes, most of the cakes in this book refer to basic frosting formulas. All you have to do is tint them with gel or paste colors. To do this, divide portions of frostings in small separate bowls for each color (if the cake is multicolored). However, even if you're tinting the entire batch of frosting all one color, do it gradually. Gel or paste colors are very intense. Use a toothpick to add a little at a time until you reach the desired shade.

Sometimes you will only want a very small amount of frosting, in a particular color. You might just want to have a bit of blue sky, water, or a patch of green grass on a cake. Instead of tinting, and therefore wasting an entire batch of icing to achieve this effect, you can do something called color glazing. This is the technique of spreading a small amount of gel food coloring across the surface of a white-frosted cake, using the back of a metal spatula.

You want to avoid having frosting smeared around the base of a cake. When you're decorating a cake on a platter (or on a covered board), slip strips of waxed paper underneath the cake, around all of the edges. When the frosting has been smoothly applied, gently "snatch" the papers away, and the excess frosting will be gone.

Another thing to avoid when decorating a cake is "crumble pox," when surface cake crumbs show up in the frosting. To control this, apply strips of base frosting with a pastry bag, and gently smooth the stripes together to form a uniform surface.

Remember to fit pastry bags with coupling nozzles before filling with frosting. Always fold cuffs of pastry bags halfway down, fill with frosting, fold up cuff and twist open end together. Pastry bags are just like tubes of toothpaste . . . you always squeeze from the back, never the middle. The coupling nozzles give you flexibility to use small tips interchangeably. You can also use the coupling nozzles by themselves for figure piping. This is a technique for building three-dimensional relief with frosting (as in Sebastian's Crab Cakes, page 179). Some large tips do not require coupling nozzles. Be sure to check this out before you fill a bag with frosting.

If you must resort to canned frosting, remember the 1 1/2 cup rule. That's about all there is in a can, so you'll have to buy enough cans to equal or exceed the amount specified in the recipe. Actually, there are some times when using a can of frosting makes more sense than making it. I'm talking about chocolate accents. Whether you're piping a Lion King mane or making faces on ice-cream heads (see Ice-Cream Creations, page 190), chocolate frosting is like the black crayon . . . the one you used most in the whole box. To make matters simple, you can just fill a pastry bag with canned chocolate frosting for "drawing" all those details. You can even buy chocolate decorating icing in a 4 1/2-ounce tube, ready to go.

Finally, I suggest decorating a cake about two days in advance. Of course, a day before would be ideal. Hectic party schedules usually make that plan impossible. Besides, two days allows "recovery time" for any cake-baking bloopers, while insuring it will still taste fresh.

BASIC VANILLA BUTTERCREAM FROSTING

Think of this as you would paint or sculpting clay. This edible art medium transforms basic cakes into fantasy creations. Just remember, you always need a lot! This recipe is generous. It's better to have too much than too little. Besides, who ever heard of leftover frosting? Certainly not your child!

Ingredients:	2½ CUPS	5 CUPS
butter or margarine, softened	½ cup (1 stick)	1 cup (2 sticks)
vanilla extract	1 teaspoon	2 teaspoons
confectioner's sugar	4½ cups (1 pound)	9 cups (2 pounds)
milk	3–4 tablespoons	⅓–½ cup

Combine butter and vanilla extract in a large mixing bowl. Beat with electric mixer until smooth. Blend in confectioner's sugar. Beat in enough milk to make frosting a smooth, spreadable consistency.
Preparation time: 10 minutes

COCOA FUDGE FROSTING

Through the years, I've discovered that cocoa is easier to work with than melted chocolate. (You don't end up with little surprise lumps clogging your pastry tips.) Use Dutch-processed cocoa for a dark fudge color and flavor.

Ingredients:	2 CUPS	4 CUPS
butter or margarine, softened	½ cup (one stick)	1 cup (2 sticks)
Nestlé Baking Cocoa	½ cup	1 cup
vanilla extract	1 teaspoon	2 teaspoonx
confectioner's sugar	3 cups	6 cups
water	2–4 tablespoons	5–7 tablespoons

Combine butter, cocoa, and vanilla extract in a large mixing bowl. Beat with electric mixer until smooth. Blend in confectioner's sugar. Beat in enough water to make frosting a smooth, spreadable consistency.
Preparation time: 10 minutes

Cut-up Cake Collection

Dalmatian Cake
101 Dalmatians Puppy Party

Crocodile Cake
Peter Pan Party

Mrs. Potts's English Tea Cake
Beauty and the Beast Party

Dalmatian Cake
101 Dalmatians Puppy Party

12 SERVINGS

With chocolate morsels inside and out, this spotted cake is dalmatian through and through. Because this breed calls for a white batter, shortening and egg whites are used.

Fig. 3

Ingredients:

2 1/4 cups flour
1 2/3 cups sugar
2/3 cups shortening (white,
    not butter flavored)
1 1/4 cups milk
3 1/2 teaspoons baking powder
1 teaspoon salt
1 teaspoon almond extract
5 egg whites
1 cup Nestlé Toll House Mini
    Morsels
Almond Butter Frosting
    (recipe follows)
gel or paste food-coloring (black)
1 cup Nestlé Toll House Mega
    Morsels
1 large white marshmallow
1 chocolate covered bonbon
1 large red gumdrop
8" round and 8" square cake pans
small pastry bag with coupling
    nozzle
#4 round writing tip
16" square cake board
    (or foil-covered cardboard)

Preheat oven to 325°F. Grease and flour one 8-inch round pan and one 8-inch square pan, or line with baking parchment. Combine flour, sugar, shortening, milk, baking powder, salt, and almond extract in a large mixing bowl. Beat at medium speed for 30 seconds, scraping bowl constantly until blended. Add egg whites. Beat at high speed for two minutes, scraping bowl occasionally. Fold in miniature chocolate morsels. Pour batter into prepared pans and bake 35 to 40 minutes, or until a toothpick inserted in the center comes out clean. Cool cakes on racks ten minutes. Invert from pans and cool completely. (If using parchment, peel off paper.) Set aside 1/4 cup frosting and tint black.

Cut cakes according to fig. 1 and arrange pieces on board according to fig. 2 (next page). Cover surface area of cake with white frosting, smoothing with a metal spatula. Use marshmallow for eye and bonbon candy for nose. Attach #4 round writing tip to small pastry bag and fill with black frosting. Dot pupil on marshmallow eye and outline cake to define mouth, ears, hind legs, and paws. Arrange extra-large chocolate chips at random to resemble dalmatian spots. (*Note:* You probably won't want to use all of the chocolate chips.) Flatten red gumdrop with a rolling pin and let it stick out of the side of the mouth as a tongue (fig. 3).

Preparation time: 15 minutes
Baking time: 35 to 40 minutes
Decoration time: 25 minutes

ALMOND BUTTER FROSTING:

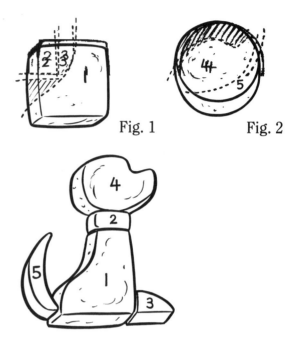

Fig. 1   Fig. 2

Ingredients:

1/4 cup shortening (white, not butter flavored)
1/4 cup butter or margarine, softened
1 teaspoon almond (or clear vanilla) extract
4 1/2 cups (1 pound) confectioner's sugar
3–4 tablespoons milk

Combine shortening, butter, and almond extract in a large mixing bowl. Beat with electric mixer until smooth. Blend in confectioner's sugar. Beat in enough milk to make frosting a smooth, spreadable consistency.

NO TIME? TIP: Bake cake from mix and buy two cans of vanilla frosting (choose a brand that's as white as possible).

Crocodile Cake

Peter Pan Party

12 SERVINGS

Remember how the crocodile swallowed Captain Hook's clock? Why not re-create some of that drama by hiding a kitchen timer in the room. It's ticking away when you present the cake and the birthday boy or girl has to wait for it to stop before he or she can blow out the candles!

Ingredients:

Basic Dutch Chocolate Cake (page 162), prepared as directed for one 8" square and one 8" round pan
5 cups Basic Vanilla Buttercream Frosting (page 164)
2 large marshmallows
gel or paste food-coloring (green and black)
large and small pastry bags with coupling nozzles
#5 star tip, #6 and #2 round writing tips
26" x 10" cake board (or foil-covered cardboard)

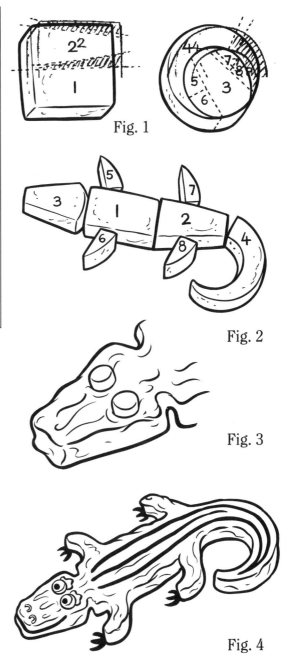

Fig. 1

Fig. 2

Fig. 3

Tint frosting green. Reserve 1/3 cup and tint black. (Tinting green frosting black is actually easier than tinting white frosting black.)

Cut cakes according to fig. 1 and arrange pieces on a board according to fig. 2. Cover surface area of cake with green frosting, smoothing with a metal spatula. Place marshmallows on head for eyes (fig. 3). Attach #5 star tip to large pastry bag and fill with remaining green frosting. Pipe ridges down the crocodile's head to the tip of its tail. Remove star tip and attach a #6 round writing tip. Build up frosting behind the marshmallow eyes and make loops for nostrils. Pipe toes at the base of feet. Attach #2 round writing tip to small pastry bag and fill with black frosting. Pipe pupils onto eyes and a grinning mouth (fig. 4).

NO TIME? TIP: Bake cake from a mix and buy four cans of vanilla frosting.

Fig. 4

Preparation time: 15 minutes
Baking time: 35 to 40 minutes
Decoration time: 45 minutes

Mrs. Potts's English Tea Cake
Beauty and the Beast Party

12 SERVINGS

This cake starts with a mix and adds orange pekoe tea for an English-taste treat.

Ingredients:

1 package yellow cake mix
1 cup strong orange pekoe tea, cooled
1/2 cup orange juice
1 tablespoon grated orange peel
1/3 cup vegetable oil
3 eggs
5 cups Basic Vanilla Buttercream
*   Frosting (page 164)*
5 large red gumdrops
4 packages fruit roll-up candy
*   (apricot or banana flavored)*
1 large marshmallow
2 miniature marshmallows
gel or paste food-coloring (blue,
*   lavender, and black)*
3 small pastry bags fitted with
*   coupling nozzles*
#2 and #10 round writing tips
16" x 14" cake board (or foil-covered
*   cardboard)*

Preheat oven to 350°F. Grease and flour two 9-inch round cake pans, or line with baking parchment. Combine cake mix, tea, orange juice, orange peel, oil, and eggs in a large mixing bowl. Beat at medium speed 30 seconds, scraping bowl constantly until blended. Beat at high speed for two minutes. Pour into prepared pans and bake 28 to 33 minutes, or until a toothpick inserted in the center comes out clean. Cool on wire racks ten minutes. Invert from pans and cool completely. (If using parchment, peel away paper.)

Tint 3/4 cup frosting blue, 3/4 cup frosting lavender, and 1/2 cup frosting black. (The rest of frosting remains white.) Fill each pastry bag with one of the tinted frosting colors. Cut cake according to fig. 1 and arrange on board according to fig. 2. Cover surface areas of both cakes with white frosting, smoothing with a metal spatula. Attach #10 round writing tip to bag of blue frosting. Pipe a blue ribbon at the base of the teapot and the cup: spread it out with a small metal spatula to evenly cover bases. Pipe a ribbon of blue at base of Mrs. Potts's hat. Flatten it with metal spatula to make a hatband. Flatten marshmallows. Place large marshmallow on teapot for eyes and two small marshmallows on cup for eyes. Pipe blue dots on marshmallows for the iris of the eyes. Clean out #10 round writing tip and attach to bag of lavender frosting. Pipe a ruffled row at the neck of both bases of the teapot and cup. Pipe a wide ribbon of lavender at the top of Mrs. Potts's hat. Use metal spatula to spread out, completely covering exposed cake (fig. 3).

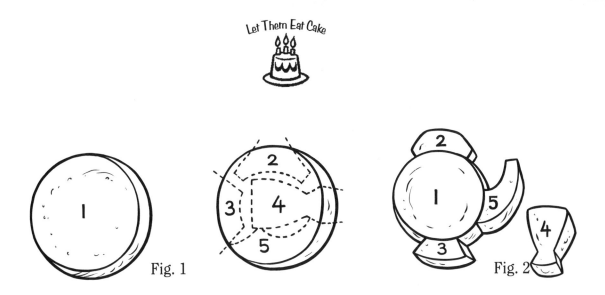

Fig. 1

Fig. 2

Slice three gumdrops in half and arrange them across Mrs. Potts's blue hatband and a whole gumdrop at the top of the hat. Slit remaining gumdrop into thirds and pinch each piece into the shape of lips. Place in position of mouth. Cut one fruit roll into four strips about 1-inch wide. Bend over gumdrops on hat like a ruffle. Overlap two fruit rolls by about 1 inch. Roll up so that you have a long teapot handle and bend into position on Mrs. Potts. Roll up the remaining fruit roll for a cup handle and position on Chip's face. Attach #2 round writing tip to bag of black frosting. Dot pupils on eyes and outline marshmallows. Pipe eyelashes, eyebrows, mouth, cheek, and chin lines (fig. 4). Outline top and bottom of teapot and cup bases.

Preparation time: 15 minutes
Baking time: 28 to 33 minutes
Decoration time: 1 hour

NO TIME? TIP: Buy four cans of vanilla frosting.

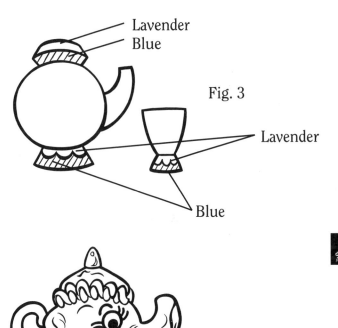

Lavender
Blue

Fig. 3

Lavender

Blue

Fig. 4

171

Peanut-Butter Face
Cake Collection

Peanut Butter Pooh Cake
Winnie the Pooh Party

Percy's Peanut Butter Pug Cake
Pocahontas Party

Little Simba Lion King Cake
The Lion King Party

Peanut Butter Cake

12 SERVINGS

This is a great three-quarter size recipe. There's just enough batter for a face cake . . . perfect for Pooh, Percy, or Simba.

Ingredients:

1¹/₂ cups all-purpose flour
³/₄ cup firmly packed brown sugar
¹/₄ cup (¹/₂ stick) butter or margarine, softened
¹/₄ cup creamy peanut butter
1 cup milk
3 teaspoons baking powder
¹/₂ teaspoon salt
1 teaspoon vanilla extract
2 eggs

Preheat oven to 350°F. Grease and flour a 6-ounce glass oven-proof custard cup. Grease and flour a 9" round cake pan, or line with baking parchment. Combine all ingredients in a large mixing bowl. Beat at medium speed for 30 seconds, scraping bowl constantly until blended. Beat on high speed for three minutes, scraping bowl occasionally. Pour into prepared pans. Bake custard cup 22 to 28 minutes. Bake cake layer 30 to 35 minutes. Cool on wire rack ten minutes. Invert from pans and cool completely. (If using parchment, peel away paper.)
Preparation time: 15 minutes
Baking time: 30 to 35 minutes

PEANUT BUTTER FROSTING

Not only is peanut butter a perennial childhood favorite, it's the perfect shade of beige for many animal characters.

Ingredients:

¹/₄ cup (¹/₂ stick) butter or margarine, softened
¹/₂ cup creamy peanut butter
1 teaspoon vanilla extract
4¹/₂ cups (1 pound) confectioner's sugar
5–7 tablespoons milk

Combine butter, peanut butter, and vanilla extract in a large mixing bowl. Beat with electric mixer until smooth. Blend in confectioner's sugar. Beat in enough milk to make frosting a smooth, spreadable consistency.
Preparation time: 10 minutes

Peanut Butter Pooh Cake

Winne the Pooh Party

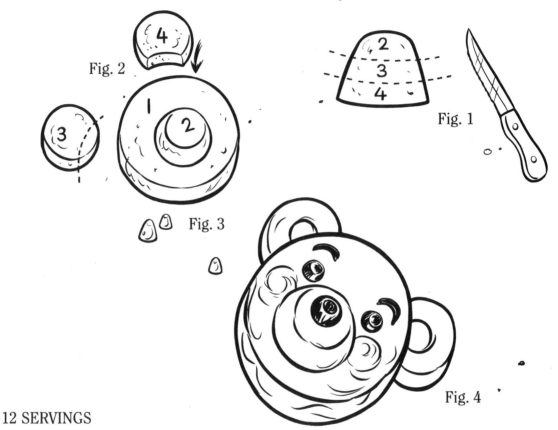

Fig. 2

Fig. 1

Fig. 3

Fig. 4

12 SERVINGS

Ingredients:

Peanut Butter Cake (page 173)
prepared according to directions
for one 9" round pan and one 6-
ounce custard cup
Peanut Butter Frosting (page 173)
2 small black gumdrops
1 large black gumdrop
2 (2") pieces of black licorice laces
18" round or 18" square cake board
(or foil-covered cardboard)

Slice custard-cup cake horizontally into thirds (fig. 1). Cut a half-inch piece from each of the lower two circles for Pooh's ears (fig. 2). Use the top section of the cake for Pooh's snout. Arrange cakes as shown on cake board (fig. 3). Cover surface area of cake with frosting. Use two small gumdrops for Pooh's eyes, one large gumdrop for his nose, and licorice laces for his eyebrows (fig. 4).

Preparation time: 15 minutes
Baking time: 30 to 35 minutes
Decoration time: 30 minutes

Percy's Peanut Butter Pug Cake

Pocahontas Party

Fig. 5

12 SERVINGS

Percy is sort of a lavender-beige pug (if there's a name for his color!). The trick to making this cake is tinting the frosting. Peanut butter gives the neutral base tone.

Fig. 1

Ingredients:

Peanut Butter Cake (page 173)
prepared as directed for one 9"
round and one 6-ounce custard
cup
Peanut Butter Frosting (page 173)
gel or paste food-coloring (lavender
and black)
2 large marshmallows
2 packages fruit roll-up candy
(strawberry flavored)
2 small pastry bags with coupling
nozzles
#4 round writing tip
18" round or 18" square cake board
(or foil-covered cardboard)

Using the tip of a toothpick, gradually blend some lavender food coloring into the peanut butter frosting. Go easy—you don't want to turn Percy purple! You just want to achieve a muddy-looking lavender. Once you've tinted the whole batch of frosting, remove about 1/4 cup and tint black.

Slice custard cup cake horizontally into thirds (fig. 1). Trim lower two slices as shown for Percy's ears. Use the top section of the cake for Percy's muzzle. Arrange cakes as shown on cake board (fig. 2, next page). Cover surface area of cake with lavender frosting, smoothing with a metal spatula. Reserve some frosting for figure piping. Flatten marshmallows slightly and place on

Fig. 2

Fig. 3

Fig. 4

cake for eyes. Unroll fruit roll-ups and trim to fit inside ears (fig. 3). Fill one pastry bag with reserved lavender frosting. Using coupling nozzle without a pastry tip, pipe eyelids over the tops of marshmallows. Pipe around edges of the ears, allowing frosting to look like it's folded over the outer edge of the fruit rolls—as if Percy's ears are flopping forward (fig. 4). Attach #4 round writing tip

to second pastry bag. Fill with black frosting. Pipe Percy's nose, mouth, pupils, and lower eyelids (fig. 5, page 175).
Preparation time: 15 minutes
Baking time: 30 to 35 minutes
Decoration time: 40 minutes

Little Simba Lion King Cake

The Lion King Party

12 SERVINGS

This cake resembles young Simba, before he reaches maturity. It makes an interesting contrast to the "furry" Lion King Ice Cream Scars (page 202) with their wild fudgy manes.

Ingredients:

*Peanut Butter Cake (page 173),
    prepared as directed for one 9"
    round and one 6-ounce custard cup
Peanut Butter Frosting (page 173)
gel or paste food-coloring (brown
    and black)
2 large yellow gumdrops
2 whole almonds (blanched)
3 small pastry bags fitted with
    coupling nozzles
#4 and #10 round writing tips
18" round or 18" square cake board
    (or foil-covered cardboard)*

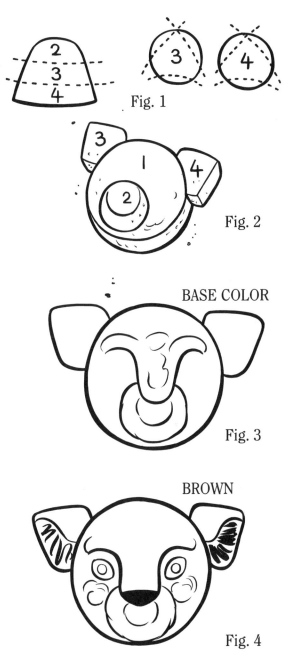

Tint ¼ cup of frosting brown and ¼ cup of frosting black. Slice custard cup cake horizontally, into thirds (fig. 1). Trim lower two slices as shown for Simba's ears. Arrange cakes as shown on cakeboard (fig. 2). Cover surface area of cake with plain peanut butter frosting, smoothing with metal spatula. Reserve some frosting for figure piping. Flatten gumdrops and mold into ovals. Place on cake for eyes, slightly tipped at an angle. Fill one pastry bag with reserved plain peanut butter frosting.

Using coupling nozzle *without* pastry tip, pipe a sort of U-line as shown, cresting over eyes (like brows) and coming about a third of the way up the muzzle. Fill in between line to build up bridge of nose (fig. 3). Smooth over bridge of nose with metal spatula to blend in ridges. Attach #10 round writing tip to a second pastry bag. Fill with brown frosting. Pipe nose and inside of ears. Smooth over ridges with a metal spatula. Pipe brown circles in gumdrops for an iris in each eye (fig. 4). Attach #4 round writing tip to third pastry bag and fill with black frosting. Pipe eyebrows and outline gumdrops. Add pupils to eyes. Outline nose and mouth. Outline line between inner and outer ear. Pipe scruffy fur on lower edge of ear, zigzagging back and forth. Insert almonds for teeth.

Preparation time: 15 minutes
Baking time: 30 to 35 minutes
Decoration time: 45 minutes

Fig. 1

Fig. 2

BASE COLOR

Fig. 3

BROWN

Fig. 4

Let Them Eat Cake

The Classic Cupcake Collection

Sebastian's Crab Cakes
The Little Mermaid Party

Mad Hatter Madcap Cupcakes
Happy Unbirthday Tea Party

Hamm's Piggy Bank Cakes
Toy Story Party

Easy Dozen Cocoa Cupcakes

12 SERVINGS

This recipe is great for when you don't want to bother with an electric mixer, or if you only want a dozen cupcakes. Basic Yellow Butter Cake (page 162) or Basic Dutch Chocolate Cake (page 162) will yield two dozen cupcakes.

Ingredients:

1²/3 cups all-purpose flour
1 cup firmly packed brown sugar
¹/4 cup Nestlé Baking Cocoa
1 teaspoon baking soda
¹/2 teaspoon salt
¹/3 cup vegetable oil
1 cup water
1 teaspoon vinegar
1 teaspoon vanilla extract

Preheat oven to 325°F. Prepare twelve muffin cups with cupcake liners. Combine dry ingredients in a large mixing bowl. Combine oil, water, vinegar, and vanilla extract in a large glass measuring cup. Beat liquid ingredients with fork until blended. Stir into dry ingredients, using fork to beat until completely blended. Fill each muffin cup 2/3 full. Bake 25 to 30 minutes, or until a toothpick inserted in the center comes out clean. Cool completely.
Preparation time: 10 minutes
Baking time: 25 to 30 minutes

Sebastian's Crab Cakes
The Little Mermaid Party

12 SERVINGS

Sebastian, the singing, smiling calypso crab, lives in fear of Prince Eric's chef. He's afraid of becoming a crab cake! Fortunately, Sebastian is safe. You don't need "the real thing" for this recipe. It just proves that you can have your crab and eat cake, too.

Fig. 4

179

Ingredients:

Easy Dozen Cocoa Cupcakes (page
   179) prepared as directed
2¹/2 cups Basic Vanilla Buttercream
   Frosting (page 164)
gel or paste food-coloring (red, blue,
   and black)
24 miniature marshmallows
1 small and 1 medium pastry bag
   with coupling nozzles.
#2, #4, and #10 round writing tips

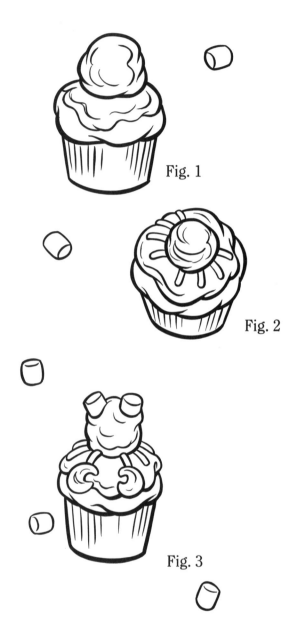

Fig. 1

Fig. 2

Fig. 3

Frost tops of cupcakes with a thin layer of plain white frosting. Tint remaining frosting red. Reserve ¹/4 cup of red frosting and tint black. (Tinting red frosting black is easier than tinting white frosting black.) Using a toothpick, apply some blue gel coloring to the back of a small metal spatula. Swirl or "color glaze" blue over the surface of white frosted cupcakes. Fill medium-size pastry bag with red frosting. Using coupling nozzle *without* a pastry tip, pipe a mound, about 1-inch high in the center of each cake (fig. 1). Attach #4 round writing tip and pipe four legs on each side of mound (fig. 2). Press two marshmallows into the top of each mound for eyes (fig. 3). Change to #10 round writing tip and pipe claws. Attach #2 round writing tip to small pastry bag and fill with black frosting. Pipe pupils on marshmallow eyes and pipe a smiling mouth (fig. 4).

Preparation time: 10 minutes
Baking time: 25 to 30 minutes
Decoration time: 30 minutes

180

NO TIME? TIP: Bake cupcakes from mix and buy two cans of vanilla frosting.

Let Them Eat Cake

Mad Hatter Madcap Cupcakes

Happy Unbirthday Tea Party

12 SERVINGS

Did you ever sculpt bars of soap as a kid? Well, you can apply those same skills to "whittling" away at cupcakes. Just pop the cakes in the freezer for about an hour and you carve them into millinery masterpieces.

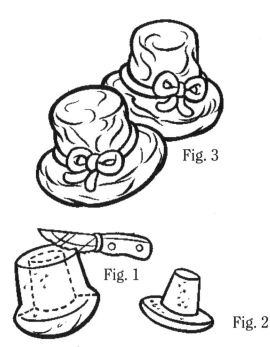

Fig. 3

Fig. 1

Fig. 2

Ingredients:

Easy Dozen Cocoa Cupcakes
(page 179), prepared as directed
1 (12-ounce) Nestlé Toll House Semi-
Sweet Morsels
1/3 cup vegetable shortening
41/2-ounce tube decorating icing (any
color) with round writing tip

Peel paper liners from cupcakes and freeze for at least an hour. (Work with about two cupcakes at a time, so they won't all thaw while you're shaping them.) The cupcake will be upside down, with the top becoming the bottom and the brim. Use a paring knife to carve a half inch from the bottom edge, a half inch into the center all around (fig. 1). Cut away at the sides, down to the brim line, leaving a hat crown in the center, which is about 1 inch in diameter. The result resembles an upside-down mushroom (fig. 2).

Combine chocolate morsels and shortening in the top part of a double boiler (11/2 to 2 minutes in the microwave), stirring until smooth. Set cakes on a rack over a cake pan. For this glazing step, it's easier to work with just three or four cakes at a time. Sit cakes on rack and spoon a little chocolate glaze over each one. Smooth with spatula while still warm, allowing excess to drip into pan below. Gently transfer glazed cakes to foil-lined tray. Chill cakes until chocolate sets. Pipe a band around each cake with decorating icing. Accent with a small bow (fig. 3).
Preparation time: 10 minutes
Baking time: 25 to 30 minutes
Decoration time: 30 minutes

*NO TIME? TIP: Bake cupcakes from a mix. Buy a can of chocolate frosting and spread evenly over the surface of cakes.

181

Hamm's Piggy Bank Cakes
Toy Story Party

12 SERVINGS

Figure piping is the key to making ordinary cupcakes look like little pink piggy banks. Don't forget the chocolate candy coins!

Ingredients:

Easy Dozen Cocoa Cupcakes, (page 179) prepared as directed
2 1/2 cups Basic Vanilla Buttercream Frosting (page 164)
gel or paste food-coloring (pink and black)
12 chocolate candy coins (foil wrapped)
2 small pastry bags with coupling nozzles
#2 and #10 round writing tips

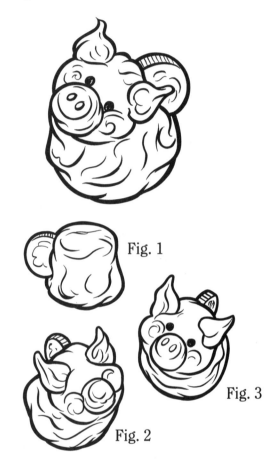

Fig. 1

Fig. 2

Fig. 3

Tint frosting light pink, remove about 1/4 cup and tint black. Cover a tray with aluminum foil. Peel paper liners from cupcakes. Turn cupcakes upside down. Cover surface area with pink frosting, smoothing with a metal spatula. As you finish, transfer cakes to foil. Insert a chocolate candy coin into the side of each cupcake. Coin should be vertical, not horizontal (fig. 1). Attach #10 round writing tip to one of the pastry bags and fill with remaining pink frosting. Pipe a snout on the side opposite the coin. The relief should stand about a half-inch high, and be about 3/4 inch in diameter. Pipe ears by squeezing frosting at the top of head and pulling away to

form points (fig. 2). Use spatula to smooth over ridges on the end of snout. Attach #2 round writing tip to second pastry bag and fill with black frosting. Pipe dots for nostrils and eyes on piggy banks. Chill cakes to set figure piped features like the ears and snout (fig. 3).
Preparation time: 10 minutes
Baking time: 25 to 30 minutes
Decoration time: 25 minutes
*NO TIME? TIP: Bake cakes from mix and buy two cans of vanilla frosting.

Cakes Fit for a King, Queen, Prince, or Princess

Magic Carpet Cake
Aladdin Party

King of Fools Crown Cake
Hunchback of Notre Dame Party

Hera's Honey-Walnut Cake
Hercules Party

Classic Disney Castle Cake
*Cinderella's Ball,
Sleeping Beauty's Disney Princess Pizza Party*

Magic Carpet Cake

Aladdin Party

12 SERVINGS

Dates and coconut give this cake an Arabian desert flair—the perfect dessert for an Aladdin party.

Fig. 3

Ingredients:

1 (20-ounce) can crushed pineapple,
  with juice
2 cups all-purpose flour
2 cups sugar
2 teaspoons baking soda
1/2 cup vegetable oil
2 eggs
1/2 teaspoon coconut extract
1/2 cup shredded coconut
1/2 cup pitted chopped dates (or substi-
  tute an additional 1/2 cup coconut)
2 1/2 cups Basic Vanilla Buttercream
  Frosting (page 164)
gel or paste food-coloring (lavender,
  pink, blue, golden yellow)
blue colored sugar
3 small pastry bags and coupling nozzles
#48 ribbon tip, #4 and #10 round
  writing tips
15" x 12" cake board (or foil-covered
  cardboard)

Preheat oven to 350°F. Grease and flour a 13" x 9" cake pan, or line with baking parchment. Combine pineapple (with juice), flour, sugar, baking soda, oil, eggs, and coconut extract in a large mixing bowl. Beat at medium speed for 30 seconds, scraping bowl constantly until blended. Beat at high speed for two minutes, scraping bowl occasionally. Stir in shredded coconut and dates. Pour into prepared pan and bake 35 to 40 minutes, or until a toothpick inserted in the center comes out clean. Cool cake on rack ten minutes. Invert from pan and cool completely. (If using parchment, peel off paper.) Spread sides of cake with about 1/2 cup of plain (white) frosting. Tint 1 cup of frosting lavender, 1/4 cup of frosting pink, 1/4 cup frosting blue, and 1/2 cup frosting golden yellow. Spread lavender frosting over the top of the cake to edges. (If you have any leftover lavender frosting, mix it into the blue frosting.)

Cover ends of cake around all four sides with strips of waxed paper, about 2 inches from the edges. With spoon, evenly sprinkle blue sugar over exposed center of cake. Peel away waxed paper strips (fig. 1). Fill each pastry bag with pink, blue, or yellow frosting. Attach #10 round writing tip to pink frosting bag. Pipe flame design at ends of blue field on cake. Clean tip and attach to blue frosting bag. Pipe squiggle design along sides of blue field on cake (fig. 2). Attach #48 ribbon tip to yellow frosting bag. Pipe around edge of cake and border of blue field (with smooth side of tip facing up). Remove ribbon tip and attach #4 round writing tip to yellow frosting bag. Pipe out what looks like small squiggly balls of yarn and fringe at the corners of the cake, resembling tassels. If you have any yellow frosting left, add decorative designs to the inside corners of the blue field and a magic lamp in the center (fig. 3).

Preparation time: 15 minutes
Baking time: 35 to 40 minutes
Decoration time: 40 minutes

NO TIME? TIP: Bake cake from a mix and purchase two cans of vanilla frosting.

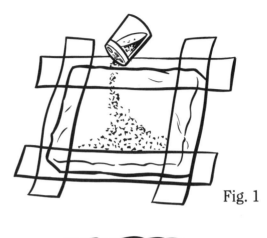

Fig. 1

Fig. 2

King of Fools Crown Cake
Hunchback of Notre Dame Party

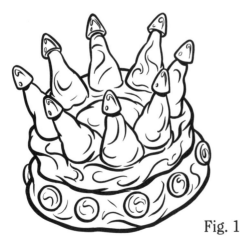

Fig. 1

12 SERVINGS

You could say this crown is made of "five-karat gold," because that's about how many carrots are in the batter. Of course, you can use any type of batter your child likes. And, if you prefer, you can always use a mix.

Ingredients:

1 cup sugar
1/2 cup firmly packed brown sugar
3/4 cup vegetable oil
3 eggs
1 tablespoon grated lemon peel
2 cups all-purpose flour
1 teaspoon cinnamon
1/2 teaspoon nutmeg
1 teaspoon baking soda
1 teaspoon vanilla extract
1/2 teaspoon salt
3 cups shredded carrots (about 5)
1 cup golden raisins (optional)
5 cups Basic Vanilla Buttercream
 Frosting (page 164)
8 sugar cones (pointed ice-cream cones)
gel or paste food-coloring (golden
 yellow and violet)
8 small red gumdrops
8 large yellow gumdrops (or use flat
 round lemon drops or butterscotch
 hard candies)
small pastry bag with coupling nozzle
#47 ribbon tip
12" round platter
cake board (or foil-covered cardboard)

into bundt pan. Bake 55 to 60 minutes, or until a toothpick inserted in the center comes out clean. Cool 20 minutes. Invert on wire rack and cool completely.

Place cake on a large round platter. Tint 1/2 cup of frosting violet, and reserve for band of crown. Tint remaining frosting golden yellow. Cover cake surface area with golden yellow frosting, smoothing with metal spatula. Arrange sugar cones, evenly spaced, around top of cake (fig. 1, page 185). (They should tip slightly outward, not straight up.) Carefully frost cones with a thin layer of golden yellow frosting. (You can also do this by frosting cones before placing them on cake.) Press red gumdrops onto the tips of cones. Attach #47 ribbon tip to pastry bag. Fill with violet frosting. Pipe a band around the base of cake. Decorate with gumdrops or candies to resemble jewels.
Preparation time: 15 minutes
Baking time: 55 to 60 minutes
Decoration time: 30 minutes

*NO TIME? TIP: Bake cake from a mix or purchase a bundt cake or ring-shaped pound cake. Buy three or four cans of vanilla frosting.

Preheat oven to 325°F. Grease and flour a 12-cup bundt pan. Combine sugar, brown sugar, oil, eggs, and lemon peel in large mixing bowl. Beat one minute on medium speed, scraping bowl constantly. Add flour, cinnamon, nutmeg, baking soda, vanilla, and salt. Beat one minute longer at medium speed. Stir in carrots and raisins. Pour

Hera's Honey-Walnut Cake

Hercules Party

12 SERVINGS

If ever there was a dish fit for a queen, this is it. Walnut cake, or karithopita, is to the Athenian what apple pie is to the American. No doubt about it, this ancient dessert must have had divine inspiration . . . perhaps even from Hera herself?

Ingredients:
$1^1/4$ cups all-purpose flour
$3/4$ cup sugar
1 teaspoon baking powder
$1/2$ teaspoon salt
1 teaspoon cinnamon
$1/4$ teaspoon cloves
1 tablespoon grated orange peel
1 teaspoon grated lemon peel
$1/3$ cup butter-flavored shortening
1 egg
$3/4$ cup milk
1 cup lightly toasted, finely chopped
   walnuts
Orange Honey Syrup (recipe follows)

Preheat oven to 350°F.

Grease and flour a 9" x 9" cake pan, or line with baking parchment. Combine dry ingredients in a medium-size mixing bowl. Add shortening, egg, and milk. Beat 30 seconds on medium speed with an electric beater. Scrape down bowl with rubber scraper and beat 1 minute on high. Stir in walnuts, and pour into prepared cake pan.

Bake for 35 to 40 minutes, or until a toothpick inserted in the center comes out clean. Cool cake in pan for 30 minutes. Meanwhile, prepare Orange Honey Syrup.

Cut top of cake diagonally into diamond-shaped slices. Pour warm syrup over cake. Allow cake to cool completely.

ORANGE HONEY SYRUP:

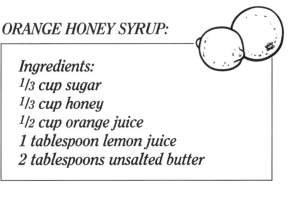

Ingredients:
$1/3$ cup sugar
$1/3$ cup honey
$1/2$ cup orange juice
1 tablespoon lemon juice
2 tablespoons unsalted butter

Combine sugar, honey, and orange juice in a small saucepan. Simmer for 5 minutes. Blend in lemon juice and butter, whisking in butter until thoroughly melted.

Preparation time: 15 minutes
Baking time: 35 to 40 minutes

187

Classic Disney Castle Cake

Cinderella's Ball or
Sleeping Beauty's Disney Princess Pizza Party

12 SERVINGS

With its tall towers and distinctive arch, this Disney symbol is one of the most recognized castles in the world. It's perfect for any party that calls for a "palatial" cake.

Ingredients:

3 cups all-purpose flour
2 1/4 cups sugar
1/2 cup shortening, softened
1/4 cup (1/2 stick) butter or
margarine, softened
1 1/2 cups milk
5 1/4 teaspoons baking powder
1 1/2 teaspoons salt
3 teaspoons vanilla extract
4 eggs
1 egg white
1/2 cup multicolored confetti-candy bits
5 cups Basic Vanilla Buttercream
Frosting (page 164)
gel or paste food-coloring (blue or color
of choice)
Chocolate Towers (instructions follow)
2 (1.55 ounce) Nestlé Milk Chocolate
Candy Bars (scored)
42 Nestlé Toll House Mega Morsels
Tinted Coconut (instructions follow)
24" x 12" cake board (or foil-covered
cardboard)

Preheat oven to 325°F. Grease and flour two 9" x 5" loaf pans and one 9" round pan, or line with baking parchment.

Combine flour, sugar, shortening, butter, milk, baking powder, salt, vanilla extract, eggs, and egg whites in a large mixing bowl. Beat at medium speed for 30 seconds, scraping bowl constantly until blended. Beat on high speed for three minutes, scraping bowl occasionally.

Fold in confetti-candy bits. Pour batter into prepared pans. Bake 35 to 40 minutes, or until a toothpick inserted in the center comes out clean. Cool cakes on racks ten minutes. Invert from pans and cool completely. (If using parchment, peel off paper.)

Tint frosting blue or any other desired color. Cut round cake according to fig. 1. Arrange on board according to fig. 2. (Level off loaf cakes, if necessary, and sandwich semicircle together with a little frosting.) Cover all surface areas with frosting, including the underside of the arch, smoothing with metal spatula. Place two double-tiered chocolate towers on each end of the rectangular side cakes. Invert remaining two chocolate-covered cones in the center of arch, side by side (fig. 3). Cut chocolate bars along scores so that you have twelve single segments and four double segments. Use single segments for windows and double segments for doors. Line edges of castle with chocolate mega morsels for battlements (fig. 4). Surround the castle with coconut grass or a moat.

Preparation time: 15 minutes
Baking time: 35 to 40 minutes
Decoration time: 1 hour

NO TIME? TIP: Bake cake from mix using two packages. This recipe is equal to 1½ packages of mix, so go ahead and bake a spare 9" round layer. Buy four cans of vanilla frosting. Skip covering cones with chocolate and buy chocolate-flavored ice-cream cones.

CHOCOLATE TOWERS

Ingredients:

1 cup (1 6-ounce package) Nestlé Toll House Semi-Sweet Morsels
3 tablespoons vegetable shortening
4 flat-bottomed ice-cream cones
6 sugar cones (pointed)
6 colored paper flags on toothpicks

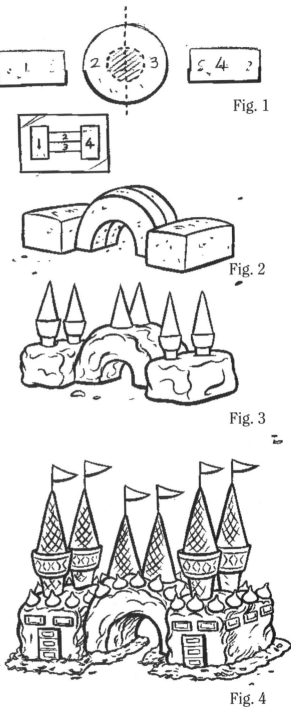

Fig. 1

Fig. 2

Fig. 3

Cover a tray with aluminum foil. Melt chocolate morsels and shortening in the top of a double boiler (one to two minutes in the microwave), stirring until smooth. Hold each cone over chocolate. Use a small metal spatula to spread chocolate smoothly over cones, allowing excess to drip back into the batch of melted chocolate. Invert cones on foil. Chill to set chocolate. Turn flat-bottomed cones right-side up. Fit four upside-down sugar cones into flat-bottomed cones. Insert flags into the tips of all six sugar cones.

TINTED COCONUT

Ingredients:

gel or paste food-coloring (green for grass, blue for a moat)
1 tablespoon water
2 to 3 cups shredded coconut

Fig. 4

Mix a little food coloring with water in a 1-quart jar. Add coconut and shake vigorously until it is evenly tinted.

Ice Cream Creations

This is my favorite section in the entire book. First, it's about my favorite food. Second, ice-cream art is even more fun than sculpting with play clay (and there's no comparison when it comes to a taste test!). You'll be amazed at the imaginative treats you can concoct from a carton of ice cream. In a matter of minutes, you could make anything from chocolate chip dalmatians to an ice-cream castle! No time (or patience) to bake a cake? No problem. Just stick candles into one of these ice cream creations. Best of all, you can even entertain the kids by letting them make their own.

Getting the Scoop

The first thing you'll notice about these recipes are that I refer to ice-cream scoops by size. Just like pastry tips, the food industry has assigned numbers to standardized measures. It's really not complicated and I only refer to two:

Large ice-cream scoop (#20 food scoop) makes about a 3 1/2-ounce serving

Small ice-cream scoop (#100 food scoop) makes a 1/2-ounce to 3/4-ounce serving

These numbers may be helpful in tracking down the scoops at your nearest cookware shop, but the important thing to remember is large and small. The large is really just the size of your average ice-cream scoop. The small is about the size of a melon baller. Both sizes should have a trigger with a sliding release that runs across the inside of the scoop. It's important to avoid self-defrosting ice cream scoops. The problem is that they do exactly that. They soften the surface of the ice cream so fast that you won't have time to work with it. And that's another important thing to remember: ice cream is very impatient—it won't wait for you or anyone else! Toothpicks are often an essential part of party food construction. Always be sure to remind children of their presence in a food, or remove them before allowing kids to eat. Two great alternatives for anchoring soft foods together are pieces of dried spaghetti or small, thin pretzel sticks.

Tips and Techniques

No doubt about it, working with ice cream is a race against the clock. However, following these tips will make things move like clockwork:

1. Always have your ice cream at the right temperature to work with—not melting from the market or a block of ice from the arctic circle.
2. Have all of your tools set out ahead of time.
3. Have all of your garnishes prepared (candies shaped and cut).
4. Have pastry bags prepared or be sure the correct tips are on ready-to-use tubes of decorating icing.
5. Cover a tray with aluminum foil (make sure it fits in your freezer!).

As long as you work quickly, you should have

no problem at all. If things do get a little soft, just stick the tray back in the freezer. In fact, you might want to work with small groupings of ice-cream characters. There are advantages to this if your freezer is too narrow for a large tray.

Decorative Touches

When it comes to decorating ice cream, miniature marshmallows, gumdrops, raisins, fruit roll-up candies, nuts, and chocolates are just the tip of the iceberg. The ideas in this chapter are intended to get you started. Once you get inspired, let your imagination go wild! This is one phase of preparation that can actually be done at the party. Children ages seven and up really take to ice cream crafting. It's an art form they can't keep their hands (or mouths) off of! When letting the kids do it themselves, have the basic ice-cream forms shaped and prefrozen. Set out dishes of garnishes and tubes of icing.

Icing, Frostings, and Flourishes

You'll recall from the previous cake chapter that I'm a big fan of homemade frosting. There are two good reasons for this: it's a major player in the cake's composition. (If the frosting tastes flat, the cake might as well be, too.) And homemade frosting is more economical than canned, because so much is required to cover a party cake. However, I take exception to this rule when it comes to ice-cream creations. Unless you have leftover frosting from the party cake, don't bother making it from scratch. You usually don't need that much, just a few chocolate lines or colored accents here and there. In most cases, there's a sufficient amount in 4½-ounce tubes of decorating icing. If you need a little more, or a very specific color, just buy a can of frosting. You can color it any shade and pipe it through the same pastry bags and decorating tips you use on cakes.

Flavor of Favor

The ice cream flavors in this section are selected on the basis of color. Obviously, some flavors are better suited to the shade of certain Disney characters. But this is really an issue to decide with your child. When it comes to the world of ice cream, taste rules! You can also substitute frozen yogurt, sherbet, or nondairy products. Quantity is important to consider. A carton of ice cream isn't always what it seems. Ever notice how you frequently can't get four 4-ounce servings from a pint? That's because most ice cream is sold by volume, not weight. A lot of air gets knocked out of ice cream, just in the process of scooping it. For this reason, I suggest buying more than you'll actually need. In theory you should be able to get 16 half-cup scoops from a half gallon. But it doesn't always work that way. If you wanted to make twelve ice-cream head characters requiring two scoops, it's best to buy a gallon (or two half-gallon cartons) to be on the safe side.

Ice-Cream Head Characters

Perdita's Chipper Ice-Cream Pups
101 Dalmatians Puppy Party

Frozen Tiggers
Winnie the Pooh Party

Mad Hatter Ice-Cream Heads
Happy Unbirthday Tea Party

Abu Ice Cream
Aladdin Party

Meeko's Ice-Cream Raccoons
Pocahontas Party

Frozen Potato Heads
Toy Story Party

Do-It-Yourself Ice-Cream Gargoyles
Hunchback of Notre Dame Party

Perdita's Chipper Ice-Cream Pups

101 Dalmatians Puppy Party

12 SERVINGS

What's the ideal Dalmatian dessert? Why, chocolate-chip ice cream of course! For extra fun, you can serve these along with Crème De Cruella De Vil (page 201).

Fig. 2

Fig. 1

Ingredients:

1 gallon chocolate-chip ice cream
12 small chocolate-covered mint patties (about 1/2 ounce, 1 1/2" diameter)
24 miniature marshmallows
4 1/2-ounce tube chocolate decorating icing with round writing tip
large ice-cream scoop (#20 food scoop)
small ice-cream scoop (#100 food scoop)

Push a small scoop of ice cream into the side of each large scoop for dog muzzles (fig. 1). Split mint patties in half and push one on each side of every large scoop (cut side against ice cream) for ears. Press marshmallows into large scoops for eyes. Using chocolate decorating icing, pipe a nose and mouth on small scoops and pupils on marshmallow eyes (fig. 2). Return to freezer for at least three hours before serving.

Preparation time: 20 minutes
Freezing time: 3 hours or longer

Cover a tray with aluminum foil. Place twelve large scoops of ice cream on foil.

Frozen Tiggers

Winne the Pooh Party

Fig. 2

12 SERVINGS

If your child prefers ice cream or yogurt to sherbet, look for peach flavors that are more orange than pink. You can also use a very golden yellow French vanilla ice cream.

Fig. 1

Ingredients:

*1 gallon orange sherbet, peach yogurt
    or ice cream, or French vanilla*
24 miniature marshmallows
24 small orange gumdrops
*4¹/₂-ounce tube chocolate decorat-
    ing icing with round writing tip*
large ice-cream scoop (#20 food scoop)
small ice-cream scoop (#100 food scoop)

Cover a tray with aluminum foil. Place twelve large scoops of ice cream on foil. Push a small scoop of ice cream into the side of each large scoop, forming Tigger's face. Press marshmallows on large scoops for eyes. Slightly flatten gumdrops and use for ears (fig. 1). Using chocolate decorating icing, pipe stripes on head and cheeks and pupils on eyes. Pipe nose and mouth on each small scoop (fig. 2). Return to freezer for at least three hours before serving.
Preparation time: 20 minutes
Freezing time: 3 hours or longer

Mad Hatter Ice-Cream Heads

Happy Unbirthday Tea Party

12 SERVINGS

You can make this goofy guy's top hat out of chocolate-covered mint patties and bonbons.

Ingredients:

*¹/₂ gallon French vanilla ice cream
    or peach frozen yogurt*
3 dozen whole, blanched almonds
3 maraschino cherries, quartered
*4¹/₂-ounce tube white decorating
    icing with star tip*
*4¹/₂-ounce tube chocolate decorating
    icing with round writing tip*
*12 small chocolate-covered mint
    patties (about ¹/₂ ounce)*
*12 small chocolate-covered bonbons
    (about ⁹/₁₆ ounce)*
large ice-cream scoop (#20 food scoop)

Fig. 2

Fig. 1

Cover a tray with aluminum foil. Place twelve large scoops of ice cream on foil. Press almond in the center front of each scoop for nose (small end pointing up). Press one almond on each side of each scoop for ears (small end pointing down). Press a sliver of cherry on each scoop for mouth (fig. 1). Using white decorating icing, pipe unruly looking hair on each scoop. Use chocolate decorating icing to pipe eyes and eyebrows. Stick a bonbon in the center of each mint patty with a dab of chocolate decorating icing. Place hats on heads (fig. 2). Return ice cream to freezer for at least three hours.

Preparation time: 20 minutes
Freezing time: 3 hours or longer

Abu Ice Cream

Aladdin Party

12 SERVINGS

Abu, Aladdin's mischievous pet monkey, makes the perfect ice-cream companion for Magic Carpet Cake (page 186).

Fig. 2

Fig. 1

Ingredients:

1 gallon light chocolate (or a
  caramel-colored flavor) ice cream
24 miniature marshmallows
24 dried banana chips
12 large pink gumdrops
4¹/₂-ounce purple (or blue)
  decorating icing with star tip
4¹/₂-ounce tube chocolate decorating icing with round writing tip
large ice-cream scoop (#20 food scoop)
small ice-cream scoop (#100 food scoop)

Cover a tray with aluminum foil. Place twelve large scoops of ice cream on foil. Push a small scoop of ice cream into the side of each large scoop for Abu's face. Press marshmallows into large scoops for eyes. Insert banana chips on each side of large scoops for ears (fig. 1).
Push pink gumdrops on top of large scoops for hats. Use purple decorating frosting to pipe a zigzag design around the base of pink gumdrops. *Note*: You can also use leftover frosting from Magic Carpet Cake (page 184). Using chocolate decorating icing, pipe nostrils and mouth on small ice-cream scoops. Pipe pupils on marshmallows (fig. 2). Return to freezer for at least three hours before serving.

Preparation time: 20 minutes
Freezing time: 3 hours or longer

Meeko's Ice-Cream Raccoons
Pocahontas Party

Fig. 2

12 SERVINGS

Chocolate or coffee ice cream makes the most convincing raccoon color.

Cover a tray with aluminum foil. Place twelve large scoops of ice cream on foil. Push a small scoop of ice cream into the side of each large scoop for raccoon muzzles (fig. 1). Press marshmallows onto large scoops for eyes and insert almonds for ears (fig. 2). Using chocolate decorating icing, pipe pupils in the center of marshmallows and a mask around eyes. Pipe nose and mouth on the end of small scoop (fig. 2). Return to freezer for at least three hours before serving.
Preparation time: 20 minutes
Freezing time: 3 hours or longer

Ingredients:

1 gallon chocolate or coffee ice cream
24 miniature marshmallows
24 chocolate- or carob-coated almonds or miniature-size chocolate-covered mints (movie theater style)
1 (4¹/₂-ounce) tube chocolate decorating icing with round writing tip
large ice-cream scoop (#20 food scoop)
small ice-cream scoop (#100 food scoop)

Fig. 1

Frozen Potato Heads

Toy Story Party

12 SERVINGS

Good old Mr. Potato Head . . . if you thought it was fun sticking a plastic face into a raw potato, just wait till you try sticking candy into an ice-cream spud!

Ingredients:

1 gallon light chocolate ice cream
24 small pink gumdrops
12 small orange gumdrops
24 large blue gumdrops (or purple if blue is hard to find)
24 miniature marshmallows
red licorice lace
12 small chocolate-covered mint patties (about 1/2 ounce)
12 small chocolate-covered bonbons (about 9/16 ounce)
41/2-ounce tube chocolate decorating icing
large ice-cream scoop (#20 food scoop)

Cover a tray with aluminum foil. Place 12 large scoops of ice cream on foil. Push a second scoop of ice cream on top of the first (fig. 1). Use a spatula to smooth scoops together around the side so that ice cream is more potato-shaped (fig. 2). Return tray of ice cream to the freezer for about an hour. Meanwhile, prepare gumdrops. Flatten pink gumdrops into ear shapes. Pinch orange gumdrops into the shape of a nose. Pinch blue (or purple)

Fig. 3

gumdrops into an oval shoelike shape. Cut licorice laces into 12 3/4-inch pieces. Stick a bonbon in the center of each mint patty with a dab of chocolate decorating icing.

Remove tray from freezer and assemble potato heads: Press marshmallows into ice cream for eyes. Add pink gumdrops for ears and orange gumdrops for noses. Use blue (or purple gumdrops) for shoes. Position remaining licorice pieces underneath noses (allowing enough space for a mustache). Using chocolate decorating icing, pipe eyebrows over, and pupils on marshmallow eyes. Pipe a mustache under noses. Position hats on top of heads (fig. 3). Return to freezer for at least three hours before serving.
Preparation time: 25 minutes
Freezing time: 4 hours or longer

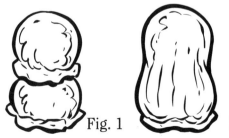

Fig. 1   Fig. 2

Do-It-Yourself Ice-Cream Gargoyles

Hunchback of Notre Dame Party

12 SERVINGS

Ask any sculptor from the twelfth century: when it comes to designing gargoyles, anything goes! Just look at Hugo, Victor, and Laverne. About the only features they had in common were wings, horns, no legs, and really *homely* heads!

All you do is preshape the frozen ice cream figures. Then provide cookies, candies, and nuts for kids to create their own gargoyles. I suggest prefreezing the ice cream for practical reasons. If kids have to wait in line to scoop their own, most will be working with "ice-cream soup."

Ingredients:

1 gallon ice cream—any flavor! (although vanilla gargoyles are rather dull)
large ice-cream scoop (#20 food scoop)
small ice-cream scoop (#100 food scoop)

WINGS: *French fan-shaped wafer cookies, chocolate-covered pretzels*
HORNS: *pieces of licorice twist, candy canes*
EARS/NOSES: *pecans, almonds*

EYES: *raisins, chocolate chips, cinnamon candies*
MOUTHS: *flattened gumdrops or strips of red fruit rolls (tongues)*

Cover a tray with aluminum foil. Place twelve large scoops of ice cream on foil. Push a small scoop of ice cream on top of each large scoop for a head. Return to freezer for at least three hours. Remove from freezer and serve on individual plates. Set out individual bowls of cookies, candies, and nuts for kids to add wings, horns, and faces.

Preparation time: 12 minutes
Freezing time: 3 hours or longer

Chilly Villains

Crème De Cruella De Vil
101 Dalmatians Puppy Party

Make-Your-Own Minty Medusa
Hercules Party

Lion King Ice-Cream Scars
The Lion King Party

Captain Hook Ice-Cream Heads
Peter Pan Party

Ursula's Icy Sea Witches
The Little Mermaid Party

Crème De Cruella De Vil

101 Dalmatians Puppy Party

12 SERVINGS

Cold-hearted Cruella De Vil makes a perfect Chilly Villain!

Fig. 1   Fig. 2

> *Ingredients:*
>
> *1/2 gallon French vanilla ice cream or peach frozen yogurt*
> *12 whole blanched almonds*
> *4 1/2-ounce tube white decorating icing*
> *4 1/2-ounce tube chocolate decorating icing*
> *4 1/2-ounce tube red decorating icing*
> *(Attach a round writing tip when using all tubes)*
> *large ice-cream scoop (#20 food scoop)*

Cover a tray with aluminum foil. Place twelve large scoops of ice cream on foil.

Press almonds in the center front of each ice cream for nose. Using tube of white decorating icing, pipe eyes on each scoop and hair on half of the scoop (fig. 1). Using chocolate decorating icing, pipe pupils on eyes and hair on the other half of each scoop. Pipe lips with red decorating icing (fig. 2). Return to freezer for at least three hours.

Preparation time: 20 minutes
Freezing time: 3 hours or longer

Make-Your-Own Minty Medusa

Hercules Party

12 SERVINGS

One glimpse of Medusa, and her victims were immediately turned to stone! When I was a child, just reading about her in my mythology book gave me nightmares. Of course, like most children, I sort of liked scary things. I just had to sleep with my lights on. Kids love creating their own models of Medusa, although these ice-cream versions turn out looking more goofy than grotesque. Gummy worms work great for snakelike tresses, or you can use pieces of licorice laces.

> *Ingredients:*
>
> *1 gallon mint chip ice cream*
> *large ice-cream scoop (#20 food scoop)*
> *small ice-cream scoop (#100 food scoop)*

HAIR: gummy worms or licorice laces
EYES: raisins or chocolate chips
NOSES: whole almonds
MOUTHS: sliced candied cherries or pieces of red gumdrops

Cover a tray with aluminum foil. Place twelve large scoops of ice cream on the foil. Press a small scoop of ice cream on top of each large scoop, forming a head. Return tray to freezer for at least 3 hours. Remove tray from freezer and serve ice cream on individual plates. Set out bowls of edible decorations so that kids can customize their ice-cream Medusa.

Preparation time: 12 minutes
Freezing time: 3 hours

Lion King Ice-Cream Scars

Lion King Party

12 SERVINGS

These ice cream characters could just as easily be made into Mufasa instead of Scar. Simply substitute milk chocolate frosting for chocolate fudge frosting.

Fig. 2

Fig. 1

Ingredients:

1 gallon light chocolate ice cream
24 yellow jelly beans (small gourmet jelly beans work best)
1 can chocolate fudge frosting
24 almond slivers
large ice-cream scoop (#20 food scoop)
small ice-cream scoop (#100 foodscoop)
medium pastry bag with coupling nozzle
#2 round writing tip
#24 star tip

Cover a tray with aluminum foil. Place twelve large scoops of ice cream on foil. Push a small scoop of ice cream into the side of each large scoop for Scar's face. Press jelly beans into large scoops for eyes (fig. 1). Attach #2 round writing tip to pastry bag and fill with chocolate frosting. Pipe eyebrows and pupils on jelly-bean eyes.

Pipe nose and mouth on small scoop, using almonds for teeth. Remove #2 round writing tip and attach #24 star tip. Pipe a wild, woolly mane around lion heads (fig. 2). Return to freezer for at least three hours before serving.

Preparation time: 20 minutes
Freezing time: 3 hours or longer

Captain Hook Ice-Cream Heads

Peter Pan Party

12 SERVINGS

"Shiver me timbers. It must be cold in Pirate's Cove!"

Fig. 1

Fig. 2

> *Ingredients:*
>
> *¹/2 gallon French vanilla ice cream or peach frozen yogurt*
> *3 dozen whole blanched almonds*
> *12 miniature marshmallows*
> *3 maraschino cherries, quartered*
> *2 4¹/2-ounce tubes chocolate decorating icing with round writing tip*
> *2 gold degres (small candy balls used for food decoration)*
> *Peppermint Pirate Hats (instructions follow)*
> *large ice-cream scoop (#20 food scoop)*

Cover a tray with aluminum foil. Place twelve large scoops of ice cream on foil. Press almond in the center front of each scoop for nose (small end pointing up). Press one almond on each side of scoops for ears (small end pointing down). Because there will be an eye patch, use one marshmallow for one eye on each scoop. Press a sliver of cherry on each scoop for mouth (fig. 1). Using chocolate decorating icing, pipe a mustache under the almond nose and an eye patch where the missing eye (marshmallow) would be. Pipe a pupil on the marshmallow and squiggly lines around the top of each

scoop for curly hair. Press a degre under one almond earlobe for an earring. Position hats on top of heads (fig. 2). Return to freezer for at least three hours before serving.

PEPPERMINT PIRATE HATS:

> *Ingredients:*
>
> *2 packages fruit roll-up candy (any flavor)*
> *12 1¹/2-oz. chocolate-covered mint patties*
> *brown decorating icing (from one of the tubes in use)*

Unroll fruit roll-up candy and slice each roll into strips about 3" x ³/4" (you should have about twelve). Trim each roll into the shape of a feather, cutting slashes along the sides. Split mint patties in half. Sandwich the base of a feather between two half patties, using a little bit of brown decorating icing to hold them in place.
Preparation time: 25 minutes
Freezing time: 3 hours or longer

Ursula's Icy Sea Witches

The Little Mermaid Party

Fig. 1

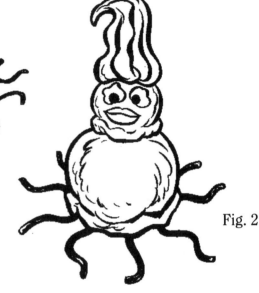

Fig. 2

12 SERVINGS

With her licorice legs and wild whipped-cream hair, Ursula is deliciously evil. However, she can actually be rather low fat. This is a dessert that works wonderfully with berry flavors of frozen yogurt, sherbet, or sorbet.

Ingredients:

black licorice lace candy (about 8 yards)
3 small red gumdrops
1 gallon frozen yogurt, sherbet, or sorbet (raspberry and blueberry make very convincing sea witches)
24 Nestlé Toll House Mini Morsels
1 (4-ounce) carton frozen whipped topping, thawed (about 1¹/₂ cups)
large ice-cream scoop (#20 food scoop)
small ice-cream scoop (#100 food scoop)
medium pastry bag (no coupling nozzle necessary)
#4 star tip

Cut licorice into 3-inch lengths. (You'll need eight legs for each sea witch.) Slice gumdrops into quarters and pinch into the shape of lips.

Cover a tray with aluminum foil. Place twelve large scoops of ice cream on foil. Push a small scoop of ice cream on top of each large scoop for a head. Push eight pieces of licorice around sides of large scoop for legs (fig. 1). Press gumdrop lips on head and chocolate morsel eyes. Slip #4 large star tip into pastry bag and fill with whipped topping. Pipe a poof of hair, standing straight up, on top of each sea witch (fig. 2). Return to freezer for at least three hours.

Preparation time: 20 minutes
Freezing time: 3 hours or longer

Frozen Fantasies

Frosty Pumpkins
Cinderella's Ball

Disney Ice-Cream Dream Castle
Beauty and the Beast Party,
Cinderella's Ball, or
Sleeping Beauty's Disney Princess Pizza Party

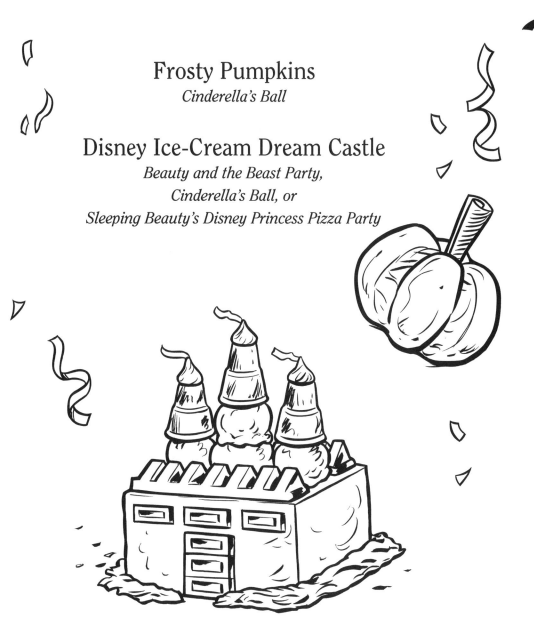

Frosty Pumpkins

Cinderella's Ball

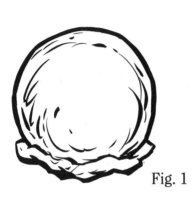

Fig. 1

Fig. 2

12 SERVINGS

If you're planning a Cinderella Ball in the fall, take advantage of pumpkin ice cream as a seasonal flavor. Other times of the year, peach frozen yogurt or orange sherbet can also pass for pumpkin color. By the way, remember this dessert for any Halloween party, regardless of the theme.

Cover a tray with aluminum foil. Place twelve large scoops of ice cream on foil (fig. 1). Use the rounded edge of a wooden spoon handle to score sections around the ice cream scoops so that they resemble pumpkins. Insert cinnamon sticks in the center for stems (fig. 2). Freeze at least three hours before serving.
Preparation time: 10 minutes
Freezing time: 3 hours or longer

Ingredients:

*1/2 gallon pumpkin ice cream, peach
     yogurt, or orange sherbet*
12 whole cinnamon sticks
*large ice-cream scoop (#20 food
     scoop)*

Ice Cream Creations

Disney Ice-Cream Dream Castle

Beauty and the Beast Party,
Cinderella's Ball, or
Sleeping Beauty's Disney Princess Pizza Party

Fig. 3

12+ SERVINGS

An ice-cream castle is the ultimate child-hood fantasy, and it's amazingly easy to make. Use it as the focal point for any of the following feasts: Cinderella's Ball, Beauty and the Beast Party, or Sleeping Beauty's Disney Princess Pizza Party. If you're in the mood for decadence, why not serve an ice-cream castle with a castle cake! Short on time? Put candles on the ice-cream castle and let it take the place of the cake. Before this dream dessert can come true, be sure to measure the dimensions of your freezer.

Ingredients:

2 rectangular 1/2 gallon cartons of ice cream (any flavor, as long as they're the same)
1.55-ounce Nestlé Milk Chocolate Candy Bar, scored as rectangles
2 (31/2-ounce) triangular-shaped Swiss chocolate bars
Chocolate Towers (instructions follow)
Tinted Coconut (instructions follow)
large ice cream scoop (#20 food scoop)
12" x 10" platter, cake board, or foil-covered cardboard

Measure your freezer to see if it will accommodate a structure 12" long, 10" wide and 12" high. If not, there are ways around this dilemma. For example, you can add the towers at the last minute, or transfer the castle to a 12" x 14" platter after removing it from the freezer. When building an ice cream castle keep in mind that you must work *fast*! Have all of your tools set out ahead of time. Chocolate bars should be precut.

Bring chocolate bars to room tempera-ture. This will avoid cracking chocolate. Know the length of your ice-cream car-tons. If necessary, trim off a triangle of chocolate from the Swiss chocolate bar (fig. 1) so that it will fit across the block of ice cream. (*Note:* Most half-gallon ice-cream cartons are about 63/4" long, 5" wide, and 31/2" high.) Cut scored

207

chocolate bar so that you have at least six individual segments and one piece with three, horizontally connected segments. Unwrap one block of ice cream (be sure that platter or cake board is chilled) and place in the center of platter so that it stands 3¹/₂ inches high. Place triangular bars along the top edges of lengthwise sides, to form battlements. Press three small segments into the front and back sides for windows. Press door into the center front of ice-cream block (fig. 2). From second carton of ice cream, place three scoops of ice-cream down the center, between triangular chocolate bars. Place a second scoop on top of the center only. Top with towers (fig. 3). Surround with Tinted Coconut and return to the freezer for at least three hours, or serve immediately. (*Note:* If freezer space forces you to add the towers at the last minute, prepare the main castle ahead of time and keep it frozen.)

CHOCOLATE TOWERS:

> *Ingredients*
>
> *1 (6-ounce) package Nestlé Toll House Semi-Sweet Morsels*
> *3 tablespoons vegetable shortening*
> *3 flat-bottomed ice-cream cones*
> *3 chocolate kisses covered with gold foil*

Cover a tray with aluminum foil. Melt chocolate morsels and shortening in the top of the double boiler (one to two minutes in the microwave), stirring until smooth. Hold each cone over chocolate.

Use a small metal spatula to spread chocolate smoothly over cones, allowing excess to drip back into batch of melted chocolate. Invert cones on foil. Press chocolate kisses on top of cones. (Do not unwrap.) Chill to set chocolate.

TINTED COCONUT:

> *Ingredients:*
>
> *gel or paste coloring (green for grass, blue for a moat)*
> *1 tablespoon water*
> *2 to 3 cups shredded coconut*

Mix a little food coloring with water in a 1-quart jar. Add coconut and shake vigorously until it is evenly tinted.

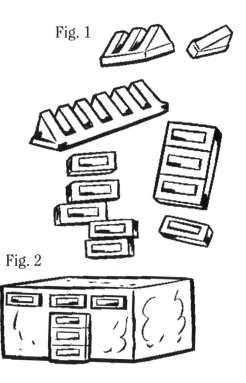

Fig. 1

Fig. 2